Costa Rica

- A ☛ in the text denotes a highly recommended sight
- A complete A–Z of practical information starts on p.104
- Extensive mapping on cover flaps

Berlitz Publishing Company, Inc.

Princeton Mexico City London Eschborn Singapore

400 Alexander Park, Princeton, NJ, 08540 USA
9-13 Grosvenor St., London, W1X 9FB UK

Original Text:	Buddy Mays, Richard Carroll, Tony Tedeschi
Photography:	Buddy Mays
Editors:	Alan Tucker, Stephen Brewer
Layout:	Media Content Marketing, Inc.
Cartography:	Ortelius Design
Cover Photo:	Buddy Mays

Although the publisher tries to insure the accuracy of all the information in this book, changes are inevitable and errors may result. The publisher cannot be responsible for any resulting loss, inconvenience, or injury. If you find an error in this guide, please let the editors know by writing to Berlitz Publishing Company, 400 Alexander Park, Princeton, NJ 08540-6306.

ISBN 2-8315-7007-7

Revised 1998 – Second Printing September 2000

Printed in Italy

020/009 RP

CONTENTS

Costa Rica

COSTA RICA AND THE TICOS

Nestled between Nicaragua to the north and Panamá to the south in southern Central America, Costa Rica has become the "must-see" destination in the Western Hemisphere for nature-loving travellers. Dozens of national parks and nature preserves are scattered like green jewels along the Caribbean and Pacific coasts and throughout the Central Valley and inland mountain ranges. Within these areas visitors are exposed to some of the world's most exotic flora and fauna, in a variety and quantity found nowhere else. Because of a compact geography that places the capital city of San José and its international airport within a few hour's distance of most of the rest of the country, travellers are presented with a cornucopia of choices. The sheer abundance and accessibility of the natural scenery and wildlife, combined with the cosmopolitan attractions of the Central Valley, make Costa Rica an unusual and appealing destination.

Costa Rica, a bit larger than Switzerland, splits neatly into three principal regions: the Central Valley and adjacent "highlands"; the Caribbean coast; and the Pacific coast. San José and the other major cities of Cartago, Alajuela, and Heredia are all in the Central Valley. The country is small—less than 51,800 square km (20,000 square miles)—so most major attractions lie within a few hours' drive of San José and each other; visitors can reach almost everything of interest without having to change cities and hotels constantly.

The official language of Costa Rica is Spanish (many of its inhabitants speak English, however), but the approximately 3 million Ticos, as Costa Ricans refer to themselves, are as ethnically diverse as the citizens of any Latin American country. The region's original inhabitants were, of course, Indians, but there

Rules of the Road

While exploring the attractions and countryside in your own rented vehicle gives you plenty of freedom, it also has serious disadvantages. Decent road maps, for example, are simply not available in Costa Rica, and most roads, both primary and secondary, are unmarked. Becoming thoroughly lost is a frustrating but common experience for most nonresident motorists; no one stays turned around for long, of course, but who wants to spend several hours each day trying to figure out where they are? Don't be afraid to ask directions. It's the best way to avoid getting lost in the first place.

Another, more dangerous disadvantage to driving yourself is the fact that Costa Ricans aren't the most cautious drivers in the world, and certainly aren't known for their courtesy. Strangely enough, this quiet little country has one of the highest auto-accident rates (and accident-related death rates) in the world; no visitor will relish tangling with a macho, intoxicated driver. Costa Rica's truck drivers also create a major highway hazard. Many have the dangerous habit of parking their rigs, large and small, in the middle of the road on a curve, then leaving to take a siesta or eat lunch. Costa Rican drivers know when and where to look for these unattended vehicles; unsuspecting nonresident motorists do not.

One alternative to renting a car is to ask one of Costa Rica's professional tour companies to arrange your sightseeing excursions, in a package that includes not only transportation and a driver, but also accommodations, meals, national park tours, entry fees, and guides. Tell these efficient folks when and where you want to go, what you want to see, and how long you wish to stay; most can design a trip to fit your budget and time constraints perfectly. Usually they get the best deal on prices, and everything will be confirmed before you leave. Payment is made to the company in advance (you'll use vouchers instead of money on the actual trip), leaving you with nothing to do but enjoy yourself.

has been an influx of Spanish, British, German, and Italian settlers over the past three centuries. You'll also notice that inhabitants of certain regions (especially those free of cultural influences from San José) differ dramatically in personality from the people of other areas. The people of North-Central Costa Rica, for example, unlike the good-time-loving Ticos from the Central Highlands and Central Valley, are a serious, sturdy folk, prone to shyness, quick to anger, and, though not unfriendly, certainly less than outgoing. And the cheerful, quick-to-grin and hard-working fishermen on the Pacific side differ greatly from the sober Rastafarians along the Caribbean.

Today, full-blooded indigenous people make up only about 1 percent of Costa Rica's population, and while many citizens are direct descendants of the original Spanish (or claim at least some Spanish ancestry), it isn't unusual to see residents with a different European heritage of fair skin, light hair, and light-coloured eyes. If you know any Spanish at all, however, this is the place to use it. Many residents speak English, but, like traditional people everywhere, most of them appreciate visitors who at least attempt to communicate in the local language.

Your first encounter with Costa Rica's steamy splendour may be at Poás Volcano, just northwest of San José.

Whatever their age or pursuit, Costa Ricans usually have a smile for their visitors.

Costa Rica's citizenry, largely middle-class and about 90 percent Catholic, is one of the most highly educated societies on earth. This isn't to say, however, that Costa Rica's economic problems are minimal; quite the contrary. Its export base is principally agricultural: bananas, coffee, and, to a lesser degree, pineapples and other tropical fruits. Costa Rica is therefore vulnerable to price swings in farm products in a world marketplace in which it does not have the leverage of its larger competitors. The unfortunate result has been a great deal of borrowing that has saddled the economy with one of the world's highest per capita foreign debts. The consequent need to generate revenue has placed Costa Rica in conflict with itself. To meet these monetary demands, it is faced with the prospect of clearing more land for farming and ranching, and cutting more of its rain-forest trees for export. In Costa Rica, however, you do not simply "clear land," for in the process you destroy some of the most biologically rich territory on earth. Today, although 27 percent of Costa Rica's 50,505 square km (19,500 square miles) is protected by government decree, the country still has one of the highest deforestation rates (4 percent per annum) in the world.

Costa Rica nonetheless remains a kind of fantasy come to life. You've read about places like this, seen the colourful pictures, watched the documentaries—but nothing has prepared you for the sight of those macaws, the call for attention by that toucan, the brief eye contact with a capuchin monkey, or the drama of the turtles and their fight to survive. The roads will have been rough, the trails muddy and leg-wearying, the bugs make you want to scream, and your skin yearns for the feel of fresh, dry cotton. But then one of the park rangers at Corcovado National Park tells you about a hike in a stream up to a magnificent waterfall where you can take a natural shower, and the next thing you know you are reaching for your hiking sandals and applying a booster coat of bug repellent—and enjoying one of the most beautiful places on earth.

Exotic fauna, such as this great green macaw, also cast a friendly eye to visitors.

A BRIEF HISTORY

Little is known about Costa Rica before Spanish explorers arrived in 1502, but archaeologists believe that the first human visitors probably arrived here around 13,000 B.C. No evidence of large towns or long-term habitation has been found; these first people were probably nomadic hunters migrating from North to South America. A few artefacts made of stone, gold, silver, ceramics, and terra-cotta have been unearthed in various locations, but the most dramatic pre-Columbian objects that have been found in Costa Rica are huge stone spheres—some about a metre (several feet) in diameter and of staggering weight—discovered along the Pacific coast. No one knows their origin or purpose, but some scientists conjecture they were burial stones. Some of the

The elaborate church in the small town of Sarchí reflects Costa Rica's early-20th-century prosperity.

best examples of these balls can be seen at the Museo Nacional (National Museum) in San José.

Arrival of the Spanish

The first Europeans to arrive here were those accompanying Christopher Columbus when he sailed along the Caribbean coast of Central America during his fourth and final voyage to the "New World," in 1502. Columbus spent two-and-a-half weeks on the Caribbean shore near what is now Puerto Limón, but was quickly discouraged from any permanent habitation by the harsh snake- and insect-infested terrain. A half-century of attempted Spanish colonization began along the Pacific coast in 1506. Settlements were established, then abandoned because of hostile Indians and rugged terrain. Finally, in 1561 Juan de Cavallón, along with 80 other Spaniards and a group of black slaves, started the first permanent settlement, at Garcimuñoz on the Pacific coast. A year later, new Governor Juan Vásquez de Coronado and a contingent of farmers, settlers, and priests moved inland to the Central Highlands. There, in 1563, where the climate was cooler and healthier and the soil rich from volcanic activity, the town of Cartago was established as the new capital of Costa Rica.

Cartago was not exactly the hub of the New World, however. There were few Indians here to exploit, and consequently Spanish farmers had to work their own soil—not something they particularly enjoyed. Moreover, the search for such anticipated riches as gold and silver—perhaps the single most important force driving the Spanish colonization of the Americas—was unsuccessful. The land simply had little in the way of physical treasure to offer, and few new settlers arrived. As a result, the colony of Costa Rica was basically forgotten by the Spanish crown and allowed to survive or fail as it would.

For the next 150 years Costa Rica flourished, but only because of the labour of its stubborn and hard-working residents. By 1700 most of the surrounding Indian tribes had been subdued, killed, or driven away, and the country's population had reached 20,000. The town of Heredia, another farming community, had been founded on the lush slopes of the Cordillera Central (Central Highlands). San José, then known as Villanueva de la Boca del Monte, was founded in 1737; Alajuela, originally called Villa Hermosa, in 1782.

Independence

Along with many of its neighbours, Costa Rica gained independence from Spain in 1821. While this new freedom ushered in a period of political instability, including various grabs for power by a series of strongmen, problems were local and were resolved, for the most part, by the local citizenry. The nation's first real leader, Juan Mora Fernández, who governed from 1824 to 1833, was responsible for exporting the first coffee, which would in coming decades transform Costa Rica from a poor to a thriving nation. In 1829, coffee became the country's major source of revenue, surpassing cacao, tobacco, and sugar.

Shortly after independence, Costa Rica also began to attract immigrants, mostly from Western Europe, who saw in the rich soil and accommodating climate an opportunity to live off the results of their hard work in an atmosphere of rare tranquillity. Unlike much of the rest of Spanish America, Costa Rica did not develop a social structure centered around large landholdings. Consequently, farms and plantations here are much smaller than those in the rest of Latin America; the more general land distribution has helped to create a large middle class.

It was during this time that San José emerged as the center of coffee production. The foreign demand for coffee, and later for bananas and pineapples, brought steady income to Costa Rica and especially to San José. British investment in particular was large, and the groundwork was laid for a society that demanded schools and roads from its government. In 1886 a law provided free and compulsory public education, and what is considered to be the first entirely free and honest election ever to be held in Central America took place in 1889.

Coffee beans have kept one of Central America's more stable economies perking for decades.

Military Crisis

Surprisingly, Costa Rica has never suffered an extended invasion or occupation by a major power. The country's only major international military crisis, in fact, occurred in 1856, when William Walker, a soldier of fortune from the United States, decided that the countries of Central America were weakly governed and ripe for exploitation. His far-fetched plan was to subdue them, then use the enforced labour of their people to build a canal connecting the Pacific with the Caribbean. He was successful in Nicaragua, then pushed south into Costa Rica, where he and his mercenaries dug in at the hacienda Casona Santa Rosa in the far northwestern part of the country. Here, however, the invaders came under the fire of a quickly organized militia of 9,000 citizens, who drove them back toward Nicaragua. Pursued by the Costa

Oxcarts are not only functional, but reflect a long tradition of craftsmanship.

Ricans, Walker sought shelter in a fort at the town of Rivas, where Juan Santamaría, a young drummer boy from Alajuela, volunteered to torch the wooden fort. Santamaría accomplished the mission, which led to the defeat of Walker, but was killed in the battle. The international airport near San José is named in honour of his sacrifice for his country.

A Changing Society

From 1860 until the early years of the 20th century, a number of important changes occurred in Costa Rica. One major undertaking, for example, was the construction of a railroad that connected the city of Alajuela with the Caribbean port of Puerto Limón, traversing the rugged and virtually unexplored

Cordillera Central. Previously, coffee growers had transported their product either by oxcart to Puntarenas on the Pacific coast, or by slow riverboat to the Caribbean. Construction on the line began around 1870, but overcoming the thick jungles and towering peaks of the Central Highlands wasn't easy. Almost 20 years later, the line was still under construction, and conditions were so bad that Italian railroad workers, complaining of bad working and living conditions, organized the first strikes in the country's history. The tracks were completed in 1890 at a total cost of eight million dollars and 4,000 lives.

Another major development that would change Costa Rica's fortunes occurred in 1899, when the infamous United Fruit Company was formed by American Minor Keith. Acquiring 324,000 hectares (800,000 acres) of rich land along the new railroad's right-of-way, United Fruit planted massive tracts of bananas, most for export, which over the next half-century would add billions of dollars to the local economy.

That same year, now with a population of nearly 350,000, Costa Rica entered an era of political stability when elections ushered in the only real democracy in Central America. Approximately 50 years later, in 1948, in order to keep an opposition candidate from becoming president, the Costa Rican congress annulled a presidential election and as a result set off a civil war that took the lives of 2,000 people. The conflict was settled after several weeks of fighting, and a new president took the reins of power. The army was outlawed, and, as a consequence, much of the money that might have been spent on military personnel, equipment, and infrastructure was subsequently redirected into education and medical services. Today, the country enjoys a reputation for its stability and its peace-loving nature; in 1987 its president, Oscar Arias Sánchez, was awarded the Nobel Peace Prize for helping to broker peace in Central America.

HISTORICAL LANDMARKS

Pre-Columbian Era Nomadic bands of Neolithic Indians visit and possibly inhabit Costa Rica. Later the region comes under the control of the Chorotega Indians. Chibcha Indians from the Colombian region and other tribes from areas that will become Ecuador and Brazil also migrate here sometime before the arrival of the Spanish.

1502 After weeks of battling stormy seas, Christopher Columbus lands on Costa Rica's Caribbean coast in the bay of Cariari near present-day Puerto Limón. He names the region (Costa Rica and Panamá) Veragua.

1522 Spaniard Gil González Davila lands on the Península de Nicoya and establishes friendly relations with the Chorotega Indians. Some inland areas are explored.

1539 The Spanish crown officially divides Veragua into Costa Rica (Rich Coast) and Panamá.

1540–1563 Costa Rica becomes an official *gobernación* (territory) of Spain. Juan de Cavallón, with eighty Spaniards and a complement of black slaves, founds Garcimuñoz, the first permanent settlement in Costa Rica. A year later Governor Juan Vásquez de Coronado moves settlers inland from the Pacific coast to the Cartago Valley in the Central Highlands. The new town of Cartago is established as the capital of Costa Rica.

1666 English pirate Henry Morgan and 700 men march overland in an attempt to seize Cartago. Morgan's expedition is stopped at Quebrada Honda by a contingent of colonial militia.

1723 Irazú Volcano erupts, virtually destroying the capital city of Cartago.

1737–1782 San José (originally known as Villanueva de la Boca del Monte) and Alajuela (originally known as Villa Hermosa) are established.

1821 Costa Rica wins independence from Spain on October 29, but the news takes more than a month to reach the country. The official Costa Rican government declares the country a member of the Federal Republic of Central America.

1822 Heavily armed government-backed forces from Heredia and the capital city of Cartago march on a rebellious San José (which did not want to join the alliance), attempting to force the city to become part of the Federal Republic of Central America. In the ensuing battle, the government forces are soundly defeated by republicans from San José and Alajuela.

1829 Coffee becomes Costa Rica's major source of foreign revenue, surpassing cacao, tobacco, and sugar.

1849 Costa Rica declares itself an independent republic.

1856 U.S. adventurer and self-styled president of Nicaragua William Walker attempts to invade Costa Rica. In a battle that lasts only fourteen minutes, Walker and his small army are defeated. In 1860 he is executed by firing squad in Honduras.

1889 The country's first-ever popular elections are held. In San José, 10,000 armed citizens take to the streets to demonstrate their commitment to democracy.

1899 The United Fruit Company (La Yunai) is founded. Costa Rica become the world's leading producer of bananas. Elections firmly establish democracy

1941 Costa Rica declares war on Japan several hours before the United States does. The country also declares war on Germany and Italy.

1948 The Costa Rican army is abolished.

1955 Eight hundred well-armed rebels invade Costa Rica from Nicaragua. With the help of four fighter aircraft sent by the United States, volunteer Costa Rican forces drive the invaders back into Nicaragua within two weeks.

1978–1979 Nicaragua closes its border with Costa Rica. Northern Costa Rica serves as a base for American-supported Sandinistas operating in Nicaragua.

1987 Costa Rican president Oscar Arias Sánchez wins the Nobel Peace Prize. The Guápiles Highway, linking San José with the Caribbean city of Puerto Limón, is opened.

1991 A major earthquake destroys much of Puerto Limón and the southern Caribbean coast, killing 45 people.

WHERE TO GO

Costa Rica has come to be hailed as a superb Central American travel destination, bursting as it is with dramatic volcanoes, beautiful beaches, and unexplored rain forests. Even for hard-core outdoor enthusiasts, however, a few days exploring the capital of San José and its historical, anthropological, and artistic attractions is well worth the time spent.

SAN JOSE

Though sparkling clean and surrounded by towering, cloud-draped mountains, San José often shatters the travel-brochure images that first-time visitors may have consumed. Traffic is a real mess, and the architecture in general is far from impressive. Street signs are in short supply, buildings are generally

All roads lead to San José, and most Ticos arrive here from the countryside by bus, the mainstay of public transport.

not numbered, and most residents don't even know the names of the streets. Directions are often given using such reference points as buildings, shops, parks, and even trees.

Initial impressions here are misleading, however, and San José deserves more than a one-night stand before you strike out for the natural wonders elsewhere in the country. The city heartily welcomes visitors, and most Josefinos will urge you to set aside a few days to cut through the urban façade of North American fast-food joints and States-style marketing ploys. If you do, you will enjoy some truly intriguing attractions in this capital city of some 300,000 Ticos.

The Avenida Central Area

Pura vida (literally "the good life") is also the affectionate local expression for "terrific" or "great." An excellent place to get a feeling for Costa Rican *pura vida* is the **Plaza de la Cultura,** the heart of the city (between Avenida Central and Avenida 2, and Calles 3 and 5). Sitting at a patio table under a white umbrella at the Café Parisienne, in front of the 62-year-old, colonial-style Gran Hotel overlooking the plaza and the open-air crafts market, you may feel as if you have taken a page out of Hemingway's *The Sun Also Rises.* The pulse is passionate and heady.

The plaza around the hotel is laid out in a maze of tiny, roofless stalls, where vendors sell everything from hand-carved clay masks and Guatemalan belts to hammocks and T-shirts. Musicians may be playing old wooden marimbas over the buzz of the crowd, while steaming plates of *gallo pinto* (rice and black beans) and heaping bowls of fresh fruit are served to travellers, chatting Josefinos, and a congregation of other entertaining characters.

Using the Gran Hotel and the Plaza de la Cultura as central landmarks, you'll find that the San José puzzle falls neatly into

The Teatro Nacional, built by culture-starved coffee barons, enjoys pride of place in San José.

place, piece by piece. A few feet to the east of the hotel, facing the plaza, is the spectacular and richly ornamented **Teatro Nacional,** the pride of San José. Designed in the style of the old Paris Opera, the theatre is where President Kennedy met with the Conference of Central American Presidents in March 1963, a few months before his assassination. Presidents Bush and Reagan have also been in attendance here.

The 19th-century coffee barons, starved for culture, asked the government to tax their exported coffee to generate funds to build a theatre that would attract well-known performers. The tax was a cultural boon, and the theatre is proudly called a jewel floating in a cup of coffee. Completed in 1897, the building has elegant floors and staircases of Italian Carrara marble, detailed murals, crystal from Venice, and paneling of precious Costa Rican hardwoods. On the second level of the vestibule is a ceiling painting by Italian artist Aleardo Villa, entitled *Alegoría* (Allegory), that depicts, in vibrant colour and detail, bananas and coffee being harvested and loaded onto cargo boats in the Caribbean port city of Limón. Tour guides, with great panache, like to point out Villa's obvious errors, such as the coffee pickers stooping to gather beans from bushes (coffee beans grow on trees).

After visiting the theatre, step into the Old World-style **Café del Teatro** for a refreshment. Used during performance intermissions, the café is an extension of the theatre and just as elaborate, with marble floors, large ceiling murals, and draped windows opening onto the plaza.

North across the plaza from the Gran Hotel, past hammock vendors and begging pigeons near Calle 5, is the walk-down entrance for the **Museo de Oro** (Gold Museum), which is located underneath the Plaza de la Cultura. A sweeping marble stairway leads to a bottom floor and a dark room with thick vault doors and armed guards at the ready. This phenomenal collection, owned by the Banco Central de Costa Rica, is a dazzling permanent exhibit of more than 20,000 troy ounces of pre-Columbian art pieces—a one-stop education in the history of gold and its relationship to the native Costa Ricans and everyday life in pre-Columbian Central America.

Although Ticos are outgoing and friendly, most don't like to be photographed without their permission.

Pick up an English-language self-guiding audio unit near the main entrance and stroll through an exhibit of 1200–800 B.C. vases, battle ornaments, large gold plaques used as clothing ornaments, miniature animals, strings of gold beads, gold bells that were hung in trees to keep spirits at bay, delicate frogs and toads (traditional charms of grave diggers), and small birds, symbols of intelligence. The exhibit ends with European glass-bead necklaces, circa A.D.1502, that were exchanged for gold by Spanish conquistadors.

Adjoining the Museo de Oro is the **Museo Numismatico** (Coin Museum), which provides a survey of the money and coins of Costa Rica, and an explanation of how the money developed in conjunction with the country's history. The long, narrow room, also with thick vault doors, has large, well-lit Spanish-language information panels and rare photos to complement displays of coins dating to 1469 and examples of the country's colourful paper money, first issued in 1864. It is open Fridays, Saturdays, and Sundays.

Walk back up the stairs, turn left to Avenida Central, and walk right (east) six blocks to the Museo Nacional and **Bellavista Fortress,** just east of Plaza de la Democracia between Calles 15 and 17. The fortress, built around 1870 as the headquarters and barracks for the Costa Rican army, was converted in 1948 (the year the army was banned) into the Museo Nacional (National Museum). Bellavista, which means "pretty view," is an apt name. The fortress is located on a hill overlooking the city, and its grounds and interior courtyard are beautifully landscaped with flowering bushes and shade trees.

Signs:
entrada - entrance/
salida - exit

The **Museo Nacional** displays pre-Columbian treasures from the Americas, such as ceremonial pots, *metates* (stones for grinding grain) carved from volcanic rock, colonial furniture, exhibits on the history of the Costa Rican people, and vivid oil portraits of conquistadors Juan de Cavallón and Juan Vásquez de Coronado. Objects of jade and delicately wrought gold figurines are displayed in a dimly lit watchtower.

The meticulously groomed patio area contains ancient stone balls from an unknown culture, almost perfectly shaped and carved without metal tools. A spectacular Costa Rican archaeological find, the stone spheres might have served as landmarks on the old trade routes that crisscrossed the country, or as religious symbols or burial-ground markers.

From the back of the museum there is a splendid view of the city, framed on the left by the Cordillera de Talamanca and on

Housed in the Bellavista Fortress, the Museo Nacional is dedicated to showing off the national heritage.

the right by the Cordillera Central, both often shaded by billowing clouds that play hide-and-seek with the towering peaks. Below is the Plaza de la Democracia, where visiting presidents were greeted during the Hemispheric Summit in 1989.

Hail a cab at the Museo Nacional and pop over to the **Museo de Jade** (Jade Museum), northeast of Parque Morazán (on the eleventh floor of the bustling Instituto Nacional de Seguros building on Calle 9 at Avenida 7). The tall landmark building is easy to spot. From the eleventh floor, gaze down on the peaceful muddle of tin and tile roofs, then look outward to see most of the city and the surrounding volcanoes. Billed as the only institution in the world devoted to the jade of the Americas, the museum includes such treasures as jade pieces traded by the Olmecs from Mexico, and Mayan carvings of owls, winged bats, and other motifs.

The **Museo de Jade** integrates informative relief wall maps, colour photo panels, ceramic vases displayed openly on a table, and hundreds of jade pieces that illustrate the history of the early indigenous Costa Rican people. Numerous old jade pieces have been found in Costa Rica, but jade quarries within the country remain elusive; Guatemala's Motagua river valley is the only known Central American source of jade. Much of the museum's jade collection came from looted ancient grave sites and was purchased by the museum from private collec-

San José Attractions

Teatro Nacional. Richly appointed and ornamented 1897 theatre at the Plaza de la Cultura. Open for visiting Monday–Saturday from 9:00 A.M. to 5:00 P.M.; Sunday 10:00 A.M.–5:00 P.M. Admission $2.50. (Page 22)

Museo de Oro. Plaza de la Cultura area. A dazzling exhibit of gold pre-Columbian art objects from Central America, dating from 1200 B.C. to A.D. 1502. Open Tuesday –Sunday from 10:00 A.M. to 4:30 P.M. Admission $5.00. (Page 23)

Museo Nacional (Bellavista Fortress). Plaza de la Democracia area. Pre-Columbian treasures from the Americas, in the 1870 Bellavista Fortress on a hill overlooking the city. Open Tuesday–Sunday from 8:30 A.M. to 4:30 P.M. Admission $2.00. (Page 24)

Museo de Jade. Northeast of Parque Morazán. The only institution in the world devoted to jade objects from the Americas. Open weekdays from 8:30 A.M. to 4:30 P.M. Closed Weekends. Admission $2.00. (Page 25)

Museo de Arte Costarricense. Eastern edge of Parque La Sabana. A showcase for post-Columbian Costa Rican art, housed in an impressive colonial-style structure. Open Tuesday–Sunday from 10:00 A.M. to 5:00 P.M. Admission $2.00. (Page 27)

tors. (Today it is illegal to sell jade in Costa Rica, though occasionally jade jewellery is offered for sale in the city's shops.)

La Sabana Park Area

At the western end of Paseo Colón, where Calle 42 forms the eastern edge of La Sabana Park, is the splendid **Museo de Arte Costarricense** (Museum of Costa Rican Art), easily reached by city bus or cab. The building, a gorgeous colonial-style structure that until 1955 was the old international airport's terminal, was proudly converted into what amounts to a national treasure. In 1978, it opened as a showcase for Costa Rican artists.

Inside the museum, the main art salon features works of 20th-century artists, including large murals by the great Francisco Amighetti, the works of Fernando Carballo and Rudy Espinoza, and humorous drawings by Max Jiménez, who depicted his fellow Ticos with a sharp pen. Don't miss the second-floor Salón Dorado, encircled by Louis Feron's 1940 wall relief mural depicting Costa Rica's beginnings.

From the Museo de Arte you can see **Parque la Sabana** (La Sabana Park), a maze of trees and open grassy areas where Tico families lay out picnics and let the kids romp. La Sabana, an important reference and directional landmark—similar to Mexico City's Chapultepec Park and New York City's Central Park—is filled on weekends with joggers, bicyclists, tennis players, and other sports enthusiasts. La Sabana also has an Olympic-size swimming pool, soccer and baseball fields, handball courts, walking trails, and a small lake.

AROUND SAN JOSE

Located more or less in the center of the Costa Rica, San José is surrounded by destinations that make for rewarding excursions. After a few days exploring the metropolitan area, you'll find the following one-day trips out of the city a splendid change of pace. Rental cars are available at numerous San José locations, but most visitors prefer to go by tour bus; your hotel can arrange for pickup and delivery upon request.

East and South of San José

An excursion to Irazú Volcano National Park and the Orosí Valley begins by heading southeast from San José on the road to Cartago. The drive from city to summit takes about an hour and a half.

One of a chain of volcanos that forms the spine of Central America, **Irazú Volcano** towers 3,434 metres (11,266 feet) above sea level, and is often half-hidden in clouds. Route 8, a two-lane, switch-backing road leading to the volcano's summit from Cartago, is ranked among Costa Rica's most spectacular drives. Look down into the misty clouds below and you'll see carpets of potato fields and hilly green fern forests, and farmers working on the steep slopes of the volcano where only mountain sheep should tread. Far below lies the tiny checkerboard that is the city of Cartago.

The 2,430-hectare (6,000-acre) **Irazú Volcano National Park** (open 8:00 A.M. to 4:00 P.M.) is a stark moonscape of sheer-sided craters with an odiferous greenish-yellow lake of rainwater in the bottom. An active caldera, this awesome giant measures more than 488 metres (1,601 feet) across and 300 metres (984 feet) deep. It is carefully monitored by scientists, who close the park and roads at the first hint of volcanic trouble.

Visitors can traverse a gravel path across the hardened lava bed to crater overviews. There's no hiking or bird-watching here, just a dramatic, up-close look at nature's raw power. In March 1963, the year the presidents of the Central American nations met with John F. Kennedy in San José, Irazú erupted, blanketing more than 650 square km (250 square miles) with a thick covering of ash, and causing farm losses in the millions of dollars. The upside of the eruption was that the ash replenished the soil with minerals that help plants and crops thrive.

Once you've looked around, head back down the mountain to **Cartago.** This ancient colonial capital, founded in 1563 by Juan Vásquez de Coronado, lies 23 km (14 miles) east of San José and 30 km (19 miles) from the Irazú summit. Over the years, earthquakes have humbled the city (a massive tremor in 1910 destroyed most of the town, including the Central American Peace Palace, home of the Central American Court of Justice), yet it continues to rebuild and bustle. Today, the countryside around Cartago produces some of the world's richest coffee beans.

For reasons unknown, most Ticos are wild, macho, and dangerous drivers (tour-bus drivers generally excepted). Don't plan to drive in Costa Rica.

The major point of interest here is the **Basilica de Nuestra Señora de los Angeles,** with its statue of La Virgen de los Angeles, patron saint of Costa Rica. On August 2 each year, thousands of pilgrims come to the basilica to pray to *La Negrita,* or the "Black Virgin," symbol of hope and salvation throughout Costa Rica. Those hundreds who have experienced instant miracle cures have left behind such testimonials as crutches, wheelchairs, and personal notes with attached photos.

After a stop in Cartago, follow the signs for the town of **Paraíso** and the beginning of a 22-km (14-mile) circle drive that loops through the **Orosí Valley,** a magical place to visit with camera or paintbrush and easel and a good pair of hiking boots. The road leads south into the valley's maw to the town of Orosí itself, a community literally engulfed in greenery, lush plantations, and ancient, cloud-covered volcano peaks. In the center of town you'll find the white adobe, brick-floored **Parro-**

quia San José de Orosí—the country's oldest (1735) church still in use—and the adjoining Museo Franciscano. The latter, a thick-walled, fortress-like monastery established in 1699, displays religious statuary and holy garments, musty leather chairs, heavy furniture, and large oil portraits.

To visit the nearby Talamanca Mountains and **Tapantí National Wildlife Reserve,** head southeast through the upper Orosí Valley to the village of Río Macho. From here an all-weather bumpy gravel road will take you to Purisil Tapantí, and the reserve's entrance.

The 5,098-hectare (12,588-acre) park is a dense evergreen forest dotted with orchids, mosses, bromeliads, vines, and giant, umbrella-leafed gunnera plants. A few marked trails exist, but hiking is limited (much of the southern and eastern sections of the reserve are unexplored because of the thick evergreen coverage and the rough terrain). The park abounds with bird life. An exhibit room with displays of the park's

At almost 3,500 metres (11,500 feet), Irazú is Costa Rica's tallest volcano.

flora and fauna is manned by a park ranger. Regulars advise arriving early.

The colonial church at Orosí is one of Costa Rica's oldest and best restored.

Driving back toward Orosí from Tapantí Reserve, you can continue the Orosí Valley circle drive by crossing an old, one-lane swing bridge spanning the Macho river at Motel Río, and heading northeast along the south side of Cachí Lake (sometimes called Charrara Lake), formed by the Cachí hydroelectric dam.

Less than 1 km (½ mile) northeast of the dam is the **House of the Dreamer.** Wood-carver Macedonio Quesada, in his late 60s and known throughout the country for his "primitive" work, has created a sweet vision of life with a two-story wood-and-cane version of Robinson Crusoe's house, which overlooks a miniature Grand Canyon. The workshop smells of freshly cut wood as Quesada and his assistant carve statues and designs from coffee plant roots, branches, and small logs. Quesada's pieces are collectibles, for those with a critical eye.

The road swings around the dam to the north side of the lake and heads west past the village of Ujarrás and its 17th-century church ruins, back to the start of the circle drive at Paraíso. As you leave the region at Paraíso and drive northwest up a steep incline, the valley recedes below, and the mountains are so close it looks as if you could pole vault across the Orosí Valley from one peak to another.

Lankester Gardens, 1 km (½ mile) west of Paraíso, can be included in an Irazú–Cartago–Orosí Valley visit, but it is also offered by tour operators as an individual destination from San José (the gardens are a 15-minute drive southeast of Cartago, about 45 minutes from San José). Managed by the University of Costa Rica, Lankester's park-like grounds display more than 800 species of native orchids, ferns, arum plants, bromeliads, and other indigenous flora. Many of the plants bloom year-round, but February through April is the peak flowering season. Hours are 8:30 A.M. to 3:30 P.M. Open daily. Admission is $5.00.

Turrialba Valley lies east of Cartago and beyond Irazú on the eastern, or Caribbean, side of the central mountain range (Cordillera Central). The busy town of Turrialba, 64 km (40 miles) from San José, reached via Paraíso, then through the towns of Cervantes and Juan Viñas, is dominated to the northwest by the 3,330-metre (10,925-foot) **Turrialba Volcano.** The town's photogenic open-air market stalls, in front of the railroad station, reach a crescendo before noon.

Costa Rica's most important archaeological site is **Monumento Nacional Guayabo,** 19 km (12 miles) north of Turrialba on the Guayabo Settlement all-weather road. Guayabo isn't Mexico's Palenque, Monte Albán, or Chichén Itzá, but it's just as interesting. Guayabo park rangers assist in guided tours to the archaeological digs, which have uncovered petroglyphs, streets, retaining walls, and stone structures dating to 500 B.C. For reasons still unknown, Guayabo was abandoned around A.D. 1400, not unlike those sites of the Mayas in Mexico and Guatemala. The monument is open weekends from 9:00 A.M. to 4:00 P.M.

The Turrialba Valley is also Costa Rica's **white-water rafting** centre, but not the only rafting venue. Eighteen major rivers crisscross the country, pouring through tropical forests, along valley floors, and into numerous untouched nature areas.

The **Río Reventazón,** which originates on Irazú Volcano, is an excellent one-day white-water adventure for beginners (rated Class II-III, easy to moderate). The river float begins at Tucurrique, about 12 km (7½ miles) east of Cachí Lake and ends 19 km (12 miles) downstream at the Angostura bridge in Turrialba. There's also a Class IV one-day trip on the Río Pacuare, beginning at Tres Equis, an hour's drive northeast of Turrialba on the old road to Puerto Limón. A two-day version of this expedition includes hikes into the surrounding rain forest and a visit to a local Indian village.

Northwest of San José

Located in a residential area some 25 km (16 miles) west of San José near the airport in La Guácima de Alajuela, the **Butterfly Farm** breeds many of Costa Rica's estimated 900 species of butterflies. Besides the breeding area, the farm has a visitors' center and gardens where the phases of the life cycle of the insects can be seen. Open hours are 9:30 A.M. to 4:30 P.M. daily, and guided tours are available. Admission is $15.00, $10.00 with student I.D.

A reported 850 species of birds inhabit the country for at least part of the year, so Costa Rican bird life has long been a major tourist attraction. From the Butterfly

Keep your eyes to the ground and you are likely to be delighted with a burst of crimson helicania.

The call of the wild, Costa Rican style, may be that of a toucan.

Farm it's a 9-km (5-mile) drive west to the open-air aviary of **Zoo-Ave** (Zoológico de Aves) near Alajuela, for an up-close look at an array of the country's indigenous birds, including the scarlet macaw, orange-fronted parakeet, great curassow, and various toucans.

Tidy **Alajuela,** the capital of Alajuela province, is 21 km (13 miles) northwest of San José (just off the Inter-American Highway) at an altitude of 958 metres (3,141 feet) in a prosperous growing region of mangoes, coffee beans, and bananas. In 1821 Alajuela was at the center of a strong movement for independence from Spain, and in the 1830s was the capital for a brief period. It was also the home of Juan Santamaría, a Costa Rican soldier and hero who in 1856 played a dramatic role in an invasion led by American adventurer William Walker. Walker, who attempted to take over Nicaragua and Costa Rica, was executed in 1860. The modest Juan Santamaría Historical Museum here is worth a visit.

The 37-km (23-mile) road from Alajuela north to the **Poás Volcano** visitors' center snakes upward past small coffee farms, neatly painted houses splashed with flaming bougainvillaea plants, yucca fences, and tranquil pastures filled with black-and-white holstein cows. The smell of smoke from wood-burning stoves wafts through the air as you enter the park and travel past a stand of bamboo and a forest of ferns to the visitors' center. This mammoth volcano's caldera, 2 km

(1 mile) in diameter, has active fumaroles up to 300 metres (984 feet) deep. From the principal lookout point, you'll peer down into the crater for a view of the steaming bowels of this massive mountain. Nature trails have been constructed on a hard volcanic bed through the small cloud forest.

The **Escallonia Trail,** which runs from the crater to the visitors' center, is dotted with massive, ancient Escallonia trees. Another hiking choice is the 40-minute uphill climb to Laguna Botos, an extinct crater lake at about 2,750 metres (9,022 feet) in elevation.

The visitors' center has photos of the last major eruption (in 1967), a busy seismograph, informative illustrations of the effects of the volcano on the environment, and various nature displays. A small store carries souvenirs and books about the region. Park hours are 8:00 A.M. to 3:30 P.M.

A 30-minute drive southwest of Poás down a narrow bumpy road will bring you to the small farming town of **Grecia,** the country's pineapple center. The **Parroquia Las Mercedes church,** constructed in 1892 of metal plates shipped from Europe, is one of Costa Rica's prettiest, most photogenic houses of worship. The long, narrow, dark-red building, trimmed in white, overlooks the town park, where villagers pass the time in the evenings and chat after Mass on Sundays.

From Grecia its about 8 km (5 miles) northwest to the arts-and-crafts town of **Sarchí.** Shops here, along the one main road that leads in and out of town, are filled

A blue morpho butterfly alighting in a rain forest is an uplifting sight.

to the doorways with woodcrafts: furniture such as chairs and desks, polished bowls and plates, and all sorts of games and knick-knacks. Most noticeable, however, are the displays of brilliantly painted oxcarts, large and small, that you'll see in virtually every store window and yard. These colourful, two-wheeled wagons—ranging in size from two-inch-long replicas to the full-sized real thing—are now often viewed as folkloric art and used as decorative pieces; some are even modified as home bars, serving tables, or settings for flowers.

North of San José

Rising to heights of more than 3,800 metres (12,500 feet) in some areas, and dominating the country's midsection

The Coffee Industry

For an entertaining overview of the Costa Rican coffee industry, visit the 2½-hectare (6-acre) Britt Coffee Plantation, 12 km (7 ½ miles) north of San José (between the cities of Heredia and Barva). The program here usually includes lunch and a short demonstration on how to taste and drink coffee properly.

Coffee cultivation in Costa Rica began in 1779. It takes a new coffee plant around four years to produce; it then continues producing for 25 years or more. The finer coffee is grown at 1,220 metres (4,000 feet) or higher. Ideal growing conditions—which the Costa Rican mountains provide—include a warm and humid climate, preferably with sunlight on the plants for only part of the day. The white flowers of the coffee plant, produced in beautiful dense clusters that last only a few days, are locally called Costa Rican snow. Coffee harvesting is labor intensive. Students and anyone else available handpick the ripened red berries from October to January in the Central Valley, and from June to November in the Turrialba Valley. Coffee, which Costa Ricans proudly export to the United States, Germany, and England, is a mainstay of the country's economy.

from Ciudad Quesada northwest of San José to Chirripá National Park to the southeast, Costa Rica's **Cordillera Central** (Central Highlands) is spectacular. Rugged, pristine, and extraordinarily scenic, this symphony of towering peaks, impassable forests, jewel-like volcanic lakes, and glittering waterfalls is what tropical mountain ranges are all about.

Travelling north and east into the Cordillera from San José and the hot, congested Central Valley is like journeying to another world. Here, in the fragrant, smog-free mountain air, temperatures may be 17 degrees Celsius (31 degrees Fahrenheit) cooler than in the valley, and quite often drop to near freezing at night. Dense banks of clouds and mist often blanket the verdant landscape like smoke, reminding many visitors of moors in Devon or Cornwall. Home to 6,000 species of plants, 200 kinds of mammals, 500 types of birds, and 200 species of reptiles, the highlands seem a mountainous Eden.

When you visit churches, shorts, backless dresses, and tank tops should not be worn.

For anyone unfamiliar with San José, leaving the city by private automobile is always a chore. Road signs are scarce, traffic is usually heavy, and Costa Rican drivers leave much to be desired where courtesy is concerned. If you're driving a rental car and get lost (you probably will), ask for directions to Route 9 north or the road to Heredia and Barva. Route 9 begins in downtown San José as Calle Central and leaves the city in a northeasterly direction.

The small colonial city of Heredia (population 30,000) lies 10 km (6 miles) due north of San José on Route 9. Founded in 1706 by Spanish settlers and today the capital of a province of the same name, it is a bustling little community whose basic economy depends on coffee.

Four km (2½ miles) north of Heredia on Route 9 is the village of Barva, a picturesque town of about 5,000 inhabitants. It is the last town of any size on the road, and the gateway to Barva Cloud Forest and Volcano. If you're not in a hurry, visit the photogenic **San Bartolomé Church,** built in the late 1800s. Most tours organized by San José hotels stop here for about 20 minutes.

About 1 km (½ mile) north of Barva the road splits; Route 9 goes to the left, and a numberless road to San José de la Montana bears off to the right. Both roads lead to Barva Cloud Forest and Volcano, but the left-hand fork is a bit shorter. Route 9 climbs steadily upwards through coffee plantations, lightly forested pastureland, and the villages of Birrí and Porrosatí to Sacramento, a tiny mountain hamlet about 15 km (9 miles) up the mountain from Barva.

Ticos often greet one another with formality. Shaking hands with men and kissing women's cheeks are expected behaviour.

From Sacramento it's possible to drive the last 3 km (2 miles) to the official entrance of **Barva Cloud Forest,** but only if you have a four-wheel-drive vehicle. Most visitors, however, park on the road near the village and walk (your car won't be bothered). The elevation is about 2,100 metres (7,000 feet), so unacclimatized lowlanders should take it slowly.

At the national park entrance station (Barva Cloud Forest and Volcano are part of Braulio Carrillo National Park; see page 42), all visitors—whether alone or with a guided tour—must sign in with the ranger before proceeding into the park. Hikers are welcome to wander at will, but because the forest is so dense, rangers strongly recommend not leaving the main pathway to scenic Barva Volcano. If you're part of an organized nature tour, however, the guide will probably take you deep into the jungle along overgrown trails that are not marked on any map.

Lush, green, and lovely, Barva Cloud Forest blankets the slopes of 2,906-metre (9,530-foot) Barva Volcano like a thick, green shag carpet. The highest and coolest segment of Braulio Carrillo National Park, this magical landscape might have lept from the pages of a Tolkien fantasy. Great banks of fog and mist roll across the corrugated landscape of mouldering stumps, towering, vine-covered trees, and moor-like meadows; strangely shaped mushrooms and bright-pink volcano flowers sprout everywhere, adding blotches of colour to an otherwise totally green and misty world. The volcano caldera itself, about 2 km (1½ miles) up the main trail from the entrance station, has been dormant for thousands of years. The crater contains a small, exquisite, emerald-green lagoon, surrounded by jungle vegetation, to which you can walk. If elves, trolls, and hobbits were real, this is where they would live.

Barva Cloud Forest is one of the country's most beautiful—and least-visited—preserves.

National Parks, Preserves, and Refuges

Unless otherwise indicated, National Parks are open daily, 8:00 A.M. to 4:00 P.M., and admission is U.S.$15.00.

AROUND SAN JOSE

Irazú Volcano National Park. East of San José north of the Orosí Valley area, reached by one of Costa Rica's most spectacular drives. (See page 28)

Tapantí National Wildlife Reserve. Southeast of San José along the Orosí river valley. Dense evergreen forest with interesting vegetation and abundant bird life. (See page 30)

Turrialba Volcano. East of San José beyond Irazú Volcano, on the Caribbean side of the Cordillera Central.(See page 32)

Monumento Nacional Guayabo. North of Turrialba Volcano area. Costa Rica's most important archaeological site, dating from 500 B.C. to around A.D. 1400. Open 8:00 A.M. to 3:30 P.M. (See page 32)

Poás Volcano. Northwest of San José. Features nature trails through a small cloud forest. Open 8:00 A.M. to 3:00 P.M. (See page 34)

Braulio Carrillo National Park (Barva Cloud Forest and Barva Volcano). North of San José. Barva Cloud Forest, part of the Braulio Carrillo park, blankets the slopes of the volcano. Hiking and bird-spotting along trails in the Cloud Forest and throughout Braulio Carrillo, one of the earth's richest areas in tropical flora and fauna. (See page 42)

THE CARIBBEAN COAST

Cahuita National Park. South coast. Protects a very large coral reef, alongside a primary rain forest. Nature trails. (See page 50)

Manzanillo-Gandoca National Wildlife Refuge. South coast. Along the beach close to the Panamá border. Marshes, mangrove swamps, many species of birds and animals. Admission $2.00. (See page 53)

Tortuguero Channels and National Park. North coast. Barely accessible and sparsely inhabited lowland tropical rain forest, cut through by rivers, lagoons, and canals just inland from the Caribbean that provide opportunities for lengthy boat rides. Extensive animal life—including jaguars—and nesting areas for giant sea turtles. Sportfishing. (See pages 54–58)

Barra del Colorado National Wildlife Refuge. North coast. Extraordinarily scenic boat ride north of Tortuguero village. (See page 59)

THE PACIFIC COAST

Carara Biological Reserve. South coast. Rain forest with trails. Iguanas, capuchin monkeys, leaf-cutter ants, and other wildlife. (See page 63)

Manuel Antonio National Park. South coast. Small, but home to more than 100 species of animals (including tapirs and armadillos) and 200 types of birds. Offshore islands harbour birdlife. Open Tuesday to Sunday. (See page 65)

Corcovado National Park. South coast. An all-but-inaccessible peninsular area affording one of the best opportunities for bird- and animal-watching. Ranges from lowland and mangrove swamp to alluvial plain and mountain cloud forest. (See page 65)

Monteverde Cloud Forest Preserve. North coast. Home to the elusive quetzal bird, and to rain-forest hummingbirds. Also site of the First International Children's Rain Forest. Open daily from 7:00 A.M. to 4:30 P.M. Admission $8.00. (See page 70)

Palo Verde National Park. North coast. Renowned for its variety of birds, including the jabiru stork. (Includes the Rodríguez Caballero National Wildlife Refuge.). (See page 72)

Santa Rosa National Park. One of the largest tropical dry forests in the Western Hemisphere. Noted for its variety of reptiles—including the iguana and giant sea turtles. (See page 74)

Tamarindo National Wildlife Refuge. North coast. Another nesting area for giant sea turtles. (See page 75)

NORTH-CENTRAL COSTA RICA

Arenal Volcano. The most visually active volcano in Costa Rica, especially impressive at night. (See page 81)

Caño Negro Wildlife Refuge. Almost on the Nicaraguan border. May have the largest viewable selection of wildlife, including crocodiles, river otters, sloths, jaguars, a number of species of rare butterflies, and more than 200 kinds of birds. Admission $2.00. (See page 83)

De rigueur for wildlife spotters are rain gear, a telescope, and plenty of bug repellent.

Numerous species of large and small animals reside in the dense forest, but even if you're with a guide you'll find them difficult to spot. Bird-watchers armed with binoculars or spotting scopes, however, will find themselves in heaven. Several hundred species of tropical avians reside here; among the most common are yellow-thigh finches, black-faced grosbeaks, flame-throated warblers, and golden-browed chlorophonias. Barva is also home to the legendary quetzal, or "resplendent trogan," a long-tailed, vividly coloured, extremely timid fellow reputed to be one of Costa Rica's most beautiful birds.

Hiking and bird-watching in Barva can be a memorable experience. If you're without a guide and want to stay safe, however, stick to the park's maintained trails. When hiking you might also carry a raincoat, flashlight, compass, snacks, and a canteen of water, just in case.

Braulio Carrillo National Park, officially established in 1978, encompasses more than 40,500 hectares (100,000 acres) of mountainous, jungle-covered terrain north and east of San José. One of Central America's least-explored regions, the park was created by the Costa Rican government (with assistance from several international conservation agencies) in a last-ditch effort to save the primary forest here from loggers. Except for the Barva Cloud Forest and Volcano entrance near the village of Sacramento, the only western access to this huge reserve lies 40 km (25 miles) northeast of downtown San José on the newly opened **Guápiles Highway** (also known as the San José–Puerto Limón highway). The highway bisects the park from southwest to northeast for about 20 km (12 miles).

Braulio Carrillo, a nature-lover's utopia, is one of the richest areas on earth in tropical flora and fauna. More than 450 species of birds and 135 kinds of mammals (including three species of New World monkeys), 100 different reptile species, and 6,000 kinds of plants are found in this huge, wet, dense forest. Because of the park's extraordinarily rugged terrain, however, only a few trails—none of them very long—breach its boundaries. The southernmost hiker's path, known as the **Zurquí Trail,** begins about 40 km (25 miles) northeast of San José near the entrance to the kilometre- (half-mile-) long Zurquí highway tunnel and runs north from the Guápiles Highway. If you want to explore the trail, park at the Zurquí ranger station about 1 km (½ mile) southwest of the tunnel entrance, and pay a $15.00 entrance fee. The trail itself—2 km (1½ miles) long, steep, and usually muddy—leaves the highway to climb into the forested hills about 100 metres (325 feet) southwest of the station.

Always be prepared for rain in Costa Rica, especially in the rain and cloud forests. Umbrellas are useless in the jungle.

Leading northeast from the Zurquí tunnel, the Guápiles Highway zigzags its way into the mountainous heart of Braulio Carrillo like a sun-crazed snake. On the higher ridges, waterfalls cascade from every slope; in the deep, twisting canyons below the highway, raging torrents rush downward toward the Caribbean coast. Panoramas of the all-enveloping

Hikers beware: These aptly named poison darts are just some of the venomous creatures that prowl the rain forest.

forest and the network of deep, twisting gorges are stupendous from virtually everywhere along the highway.

The park's other principal hiking trail begins at the **Quebrada Gonzales** ranger station, 23 km (14 miles) northeast of the Zurquí tunnel. Following a cascading jungle stream through towering groves of *javillo, higueron,* and naked Indian trees (the latter are easily recognizable because of their reddish bark and sparse canopy), the path loops through the forest for about 3 km (2 miles) before returning to the ranger station.

This is snake country, so wear boots and don't put your hands or feet in places you can't see. Costa Rica has an abundance of reptiles, both poisonous and nonpoisonous, but because of Braulio Carrillo's virtually undisturbed terrain the national park has more than its share.

The easiest creatures to observe in the dense forests of Braulio Carrillo, especially if you're carrying binoculars or a spotting scope, are the brightly coloured tropical birds. About 450 species inhabit the rain and cloud forests here, many of them commonly spotted by hikers. Bird lists are usually available at the Zurquí and Quebrada Gonzales ranger stations; if you're interested, ask.

There are other hiking trails in Braulio Carrillo in addition to those near the Zurquí tunnel and at Quebrada Gonzales ranger station, but rangers don't broadcast their whereabouts for a very good reason. The forest here is so dense—and, to unaccompanied amateur jungle walkers at least, so dangerous—that longer, less well maintained trails should be explored only in the company of a guide. If you're interested in more difficult hikes into Braulio Carrillo, contact a local trekking company in San José.

There are no accommodations of any kind in Braulio Carrillo National Park, so once you've completed your visit you must drive back to San José or, if your plans include the Caribbean coast, go on eastward to Puerto Limón (107 km/66 miles from the park's eastern boundary). If you choose to head east, note that the Guápiles Highway leaves Braulio Carrillo near the village of Santa Clara, about 10 km (6 miles) east of the Quebrada Gonzales ranger station.

In the jungle, wear boots, move slowly and carefully, and don't put your hands or feet anywhere you can't see.

THE CARIBBEAN COAST

When Christopher Columbus dropped anchor near present-day Puerto Limón on Costa Rica's Caribbean coast in 1502, he was searching for an easy trade route to the Far East. What he found instead was an unwelcoming landscape of dense tropical rain forest, a hostile Indian population, rampant disease, unpalatable water, and more biting insects and deadly snakes than a respectable European could imagine or would endure. The busy explorer and his small flotilla of ships didn't stick around for more than a few weeks.

Things have changed in 500 years, of course, and today Costa Rica's spectacular eastern coast—some 160 km (100 miles) of uninhabited palm-lined beaches, wildlife rich wetlands, and dense, unexplored rain forests—is one of the country's most popular resort areas. Mainly because of the remote location and a 1991 earthquake that destroyed property and roads, life here is less sophisticated than in other parts of Costa Rica, and some areas are hard to reach, but the region is still gorgeous and certainly worth a visit.

The terrain along the northern coastline is basically similar to that of the southern coast—a contrasting combination of jungles, swamps, and long, empty beaches—but there are significant cultural and logistical distinctions between the

Burning for Bananas

You may notice large clouds of smoke in the air as you head southeast toward Puerto Limón and the Caribbean; they are caused by local farmers burning back segments of rain forest to make way for banana plantations. Bananas aren't indigenous to Costa Rica, of course (or, for that matter, to Central or South America—scientists say they originated in Asia), but were probably brought to the New World by Spaniards in the late 15th century.

Bananas are of great importance to most Costa Ricans, not only as food but also because they are the country's number-one export crop (most go to the United States and Europe). You'll see these tasty yellow fruits growing virtually everywhere in the tropical lowlands: from residential backyards to the large plantations bisected by the Guápiles Highway on its way to Puerto Limón. Banana plants aren't particularly difficult to cultivate, but they do require an enormous amount of patience. After producing only a single *racimo* (bunch), each banana shoot, or "branch," dies. It is immediately replaced by a new shoot from the same trunk, but a full nine months elapses from the start of the bud to harvest. And, like most fruits, bananas are highly susceptible to insects. To help keep fruit flies at a distance, *racimos* are often encased in blue, insecticide-impregnated plastic bags.

two areas that you might wish to ponder when planning your Caribbean-side trip. For example, the sparsely settled north is inhabited mostly by Hispanics and indigenous Indians, while the vast majority of residents along the more populated southern coast are Creole-speaking Rastafarians of Jamaican descent. Most visitors will notice quickly that the Rastafarians are simply not as outgoing, friendly, or as hospitable as the Ticos and Indians in the north.

Another difference in the two areas is accessibility. All travel to and along the northern coast above Puerto Limón is by boat or airplane. Consequently, moving about here is fairly slow, and sometimes travel arrangements are difficult to make. The area south of Puerto Limón, on the other hand, is far more accessible to visitors because of the Puerto Limón–Cahuita–Puerto Viejo highway that hugs the shoreline all the way to Panamá.

And if you're a wildlife watcher, consider this: Wild animals are undoubtedly more numerous in the north's remote, uninhabited jungles than they are in the more densely populated south, but the critters are often harder to spot because of the thick vegetation and lack of roads and hiking trails. If you're interested in watching giant sea turtles nest, the beaches of Tortuguero National Park on the north coast offer some of the best turtle-gawking opportunities in the world. And always remember that, whatever direction you choose, you'll have to deal with gnats, mosquitoes, snakes, spiders, and the potential for getting lost in the jungle. Carry plenty of insect repellent, watch where you put your hands and feet, and never go into the rain forest by yourself.

The Caribbean Coast South

The Guápiles Highway from San José to Puerto Limón exits Braulio Carrillo National Park a few kilometres northeast of the Quebrada Gonzales ranger station and runs east. Near the town of Guácimo it turns southeast and leaves the mountains to enter the lower, warmer climes of the Caribbean tropical lowlands. Here, large segments of rain forest adjacent to the highway have been chopped and burned back to make room for macadamia nut farms, ornamental plant nurseries, cattle ranches, and banana plantations. Because of this forest destruction, the area is far less scenic than the mountainous terrain of Braulio Carrillo to the west, but where farmers and ranchers are concerned it is certainly more livable.

The final 35 km (22 miles) of pavement on the Guápiles Highway northwest of Puerto Limón were badly damaged by the 1991 earthquake, which reached 7.6 on the Richter scale, killed 45 people, and destroyed numerous towns and villages throughout the area. The road itself is rough and hazardous in sections, and you'll notice that highway bridges seem to be raised seven or eight inches above the pavement. In reality, it was the road that dropped during the earthquake, while the bridges, supported by solid concrete abutments, stayed in place.

The coastal city of **Puerto Limón** (population 70,000) is the unofficial dividing point between the north and south Pacific coasts of Costa Rica. Capital of the province with the same name, Puerto

The rugged coastline near Puerto Viejo attracts surfers from around the world.

Limón is not what anyone would call picturesque. Many of the city's buildings were destroyed or badly damaged in the 1991 earthquake and, like most tropical ports, the place is run-down and a bit seedy. Puerto Limón's principal claim to fame is the fact that Christopher Columbus, on his fourth voyage to the New World in 1502, spent 17 days in the area repairing his tiny flotilla of storm-battered ships. The city celebrates the event with a five-day carnival called El Día de la Raza (The Day of the People), held in October.

Puerto Limón's population is a colourful ethnic mixture of Hispanic, black, Chinese, and indigenous Indian. Most residents here are friendly and helpful, but if your wallet is fat or you're wearing lots of jewellery it's not a good idea to wander around the city at night. Local police say the downtown area turns mean when the sun goes down, and more than one tourist out on the town has been unceremoniously relieved of his or her belongings by local hoodlums.

The downtown section of Puerto Limón, adjacent to the harbour, is concentrated in a few square blocks. If you like to walk, take a stroll to palm-shaded Parque Vargas (the main city park) along the old sea wall, which was constructed more than a hundred years ago to protect the town from the sea. The island you'll see lying about 1 km (½ mile) offshore just opposite Parque Vargas is Isla Uvita, where Columbus landed in 1502 to repair his ships. (Tours to the island aren't offered by local guides because there's simply nothing to see.) Two blocks directly inland from Parque Vargas is Market Square, a noisy, colourful collection of stalls and vendors where you can buy anything from freshly caught fish to local arts and crafts. About 5 km (3 miles) northwest of downtown Puerto Limón on Calle Portete (Portete Road is the main street skirting the harbour and the Caribbean) there's a good place for a picnic: Parque Cariari, a quiet, shaded city park on a bluff overlooking the sea. A block southeast of Parque Cariari is Playa Bonita, Puerto Limón's main municipal beach.

Only one highway leads south out of Puerto Limón toward Cahuita, Puerto Viejo, and the border with Panamá. It is an unmarked, straight-as-an-arrow ribbon of narrow asphalt that begins downtown near the harbour and then sticks to the Caribbean coast like glue. The road has no official name or number, but if you get lost leaving Puerto Limón, just ask for directions to Cahuita.

The drive south along this beach-hugging highway is memorable. As with the Guápiles Highway west of Puerto Limón, the pavement here, damaged in the 1991 earthquake, is badly rutted in spots, but with the Caribbean and its pure-white beach on the left, and a dense tropical forest on the right, the landscape is gloriously scenic. Travellers are welcome to stop and swim, sunbathe, and beachcomb anywhere they can reach the water along the 47-km (29-mile) stretch between Puerto Limón and the village of Cahuita. Overnight camping isn't recommended, however. Large waves—not of the tsunami variety, but powerful enough to wash away a tent—occasionally roll onto the beach. The area is also remote and lonely; it rarely happens, but beach campers have been roughed up and robbed in the past.

Skimpy bathing attire is fine at Costa Rica's swimming pools and beaches, but nudity is not.

The beach town of **Cahuita,** 47 km (29 miles) south of Puerto Limón, inhabited mainly by Rastafarians whose Jamaican ancestors worked on the banana plantations in the area, depends heavily upon tourism for its livelihood. Among its touristic offerings are excellent surfing and snorkeling conditions, a glass-bottomed boat concession, and a pleasant, if cluttered (with drift logs), beach. Cahuita is also within walking distance of the northern end of **Cahuita National Park.**

With its curving white beach backed by lush rain forests, Cahuita Park may indeed be paradise.

The main entrance to the park (officially known as the Puerto Vargas entrance) lies 4 km (2½ miles) south of Cahuita at an easy-to-find junction marked by a large roadside sign. Encompassing about 1,093 hectares (2,700 acres), the park was established by the Costa Rican government to protect a very large coral reef from pollution created by nearby banana plantations. It also safeguards a dense segment of primary seaside rain forest that was somehow overlooked by loggers earlier in this century. The park's wide, white beaches are far cleaner and prettier than those found near Cahuita village to the north, and the snorkeling over the reef is superb. Several nature trails bisect the beachside forest.

Puerto Viejo lies 6 km (3½ miles) south of the Cahuita National Park turnoff on the main highway. Strung out north-to-south along the main road, this town, like Cahuita village to the north, depends heavily upon sun-seekers and nature-lovers for its survival. Many permanent residents are Rastafarian farmers or fishermen who double as guides or tour leaders. Two Indian tribes, the Bribrí and the Cabecar, also reside in the area, but tribe members usually stay close to their official rain-forest reservations near the Panamá border.

Along Puerto Viejo's main street you'll find a few souvenir shops, several small cafés, and a gasoline station, but not much else. The village is so small that you can easily walk to whatever destination you choose, but most area lodges rent bicycles if you'd rather ride than ramble. If you do rent a bike, be aware that the river bridges on either end of town are narrow and without protective guard rails. More than one cyclist has gone to the Puerto Limón hospital with broken limbs after losing his or her balance on the bridge and falling into the river below.

The Puerto Viejo area is known best for its snorkeling, surfing, and sportfishing. Snorkeling equipment may be rent-

Look to the Trees

The most obvious and obnoxious residents in Cahuita National Park are howler monkeys. Swinging through the trees overhead, troops of these furry acrobats often follow motorists or hikers along the 6-km (3½-mile) road that winds through the park. The inharmonious jungle symphony they create (one scientist described it as a "roll of distant thunder preceded by the death-agonies of half a dozen tortured jaguars") can be terrifying to the uninitiated. Howlers, which range throughout Central and South America, are Costa Rica's most common variety of monkey. Varying in colour from pure black to burnished gold and sporting long, protruding dog-like faces, they are nearly always found in forested areas, usually in the tallest trees. Two other species of monkeys—a small, shy breed called spider monkeys, and cute, mischievous, baby-faced primates known as white-throated capuchins (locally but mistakenly called white-faced monkeys)—also reside in Cahuita.

ed from most hotels in the area, and surfboards can often be leased or purchased from locals. The most popular beach in town is a long, beautiful stretch of black sand a ten-minute stroll to the north. The black sand is from volcanic activity in the area several thousand years ago.

The rough, narrow dirt track that heads south from Puerto Viejo to the hamlets of Punta Uva and Manzanillo and the Manzanillo-Gandoca National Wildlife Refuge hugs the coast like a lover. The former, **Punta Uva,** 7 km (4 miles) south of Puerto Viejo, is little more than a scanty accumulation of huts and houses along the road. The long, clean, palm-lined beaches here, however, are probably the prettiest on the Costa Rican Caribbean. Beach access is via any of the sandy, unmarked roads that turn left (if you are headed south) off the main drag. At Punta Uva itself (a rocky point jutting into the sea near the village), the snorkeling over a small coral reef is superb.

Manzanillo-Gandoca National Wildlife Refuge lies just south of the village of Manzanillo at the very end of the road, less than 10 km (6 miles) from the Panamá border. The main beach trail into the reserve, which begins at the parking area, is easy to spot. The 9,720-hectare (24,000-acre) sanctuary protects a large sea-turtle nesting beach, plus a substantial segment of primary rain forest and freshwater marsh. Access is by trail only; about 15 km (9 miles) of unmaintained hiking paths meander along the beach and through the forest. It's probably a good idea to stick to the trails along the beach if you don't have rubber boots and aren't accompanied by a guide.

Except for the palm trees, this rugged coast—indented by rocky coves and dotted with tiny islands—often reminds visitors of the scenic shoreline of the state of Maine. The rain forest here has sizable populations of tapirs, monkeys, crocodiles, sloths, and ocelots, while the marshes and mangrove swamps are home to tarpon, West Indian manatees, and

This Indiana Jones is in search of wildlife spotting, not wild adventure.

caiman (a species of freshwater crocodile). And, like most wildlife reserves and national parks in Costa Rica, Manzanillo-Gandoca is a bird- watcher's paradise, home to more than 350 species. Especially common here are parrots, five different species of which reside in the refuge.

The Caribbean Coast North

The northern half of Costa Rica's beautiful Caribbean coast—from Puerto Limón northwest to the Nicaraguan border—is one of the country's wildest and least explored regions. Covered by a virtually impenetrable carpet of verdant jungle known officially as "lowland tropical rain forest," the land here is flat, hot, humid, and, not surprisingly, abundant in wildlife. Sloths, tapirs, and jaguars are far more common than cattle, and the forest is so thick (and dangerous) that even local guides will enter only on well-maintained trails. Human habitation is rare; fewer than a dozen tiny villages exist along the entire 140-km (87-mile) stretch of coast from Puerto Limón up to Nicaragua.

Some roads have been cut through the forest, of course, but travel in this huge expanse of jungle wilderness is most often by boat, along a network of both natural and man-made coastal waterways known as the **Tortuguero Channels.** Lying approximately a kilometre (a half-mile) inland and running parallel to the sea, these liquid highways—comprising rivers, lagoons, and hand-dug canals that connect the natural waterways—offer the only viable access for visitors wishing to explore this mostly undisturbed landscape.

At one time the Costa Rican government operated a twice-weekly boat service from Puerto Moín (Puerto Limón's deep-water port) to the Nicaraguan border via the Tortuguero Channels. That service was terminated in 1992. Today travellers wishing to visit the northern Caribbean coast must either hire a private boat and guide in Puerto Moín to ferry them up the channels, stay at a Caribbean-coast lodge that provides its own free transportation, or fly from San José to Tortuguero village by small plane.

If you're driving east from San José to Puerto Limón on the Guápiles Highway, you will find Puerto Moín on the left about 6 km (3½ miles) north of Puerto Limón. Watch for the concentration of cargo ships and huge loading cranes visible from the highway; the access road, on the left, is marked by signs. The private dock at which all tourist boats are hired is about ½ km (⅓ mile) north of the commercial port itself.

The 77-km (48-mile) **boat ride** north via the Tortuguero Channels from Puerto Moín to Tortuguero village is undoubtedly one of the most memorable sojourns a visitor to Costa Rica can make. Indeed, if there is an *African Queen* experience to be had in Costa Rica, it is offered by the Tortuguero Channels. Varying in width from 10 to 91 metres (30 to 300 feet), in depth from 1 to 5 metres (2 to 15 feet), and running parallel to the Caribbean less than a kilometre (½ mile) inland, this network of waterways slithers through the solitary jungle like a great brown serpent. In many places huge rafts of bright-green water hyacinths threaten to choke off the waterway completely; in others, the water is so shallow that boats often momentarily run aground. Giant blue morpho butterflies dance, dart, and hover over the lagoons like azure pie plates on elastic strings,

Turtle Nesting

Of all the attractions and adventures awaiting travellers in the Tortuguero National Park area, observing the giant sea turtles as they lay their eggs on the nearby beach is by far the most popular. The primary turtle nesting season here is from May through September, but these huge reptiles can usually be seen at any time of the year. Nearly all of the lodges in the Tortuguero region offer year-round guided turtle-watching expeditions as part of their menu of guest activities.

Three species of giant sea turtles nest on Tortuguero's beaches: the green turtle, about 1 metre (3 feet) in length and weighing up to 186 kg (500 pounds); the hawksbill, usually weighing around 93 kg (250 pounds); and the leatherback, sometimes growing to 1½ metres (5 feet) in length and weighing up to 298 kg (800 pounds).

If a female is disturbed by lights or movement as she crawls up the beach in search of a nesting site, she will simply turn around and return to the sea. Once the egg-laying process has begun, however, she will stay on the nest until finished. It is during this time that human observers can quietly approach to watch and take photographs. From beginning to end the laying procedure can last more than two hours.

If the nest is not destroyed by high water, heavy rainfall, or predators such as crabs, seabirds, or human beings, the eggs will hatch in about two months, after which the 5-cm- (2-inch-) long baby turtles make a dash for the nearby sea. Many are taken by predators seconds after leaving the nest; those that do reach the water are at the mercy of fish, sea currents, and a hundred other dangers.

During the peak of the nesting season it's against the law to be on the beach at night without a guide and an official permit. The latter is available at a modest fee from the national park office in Tortuguero village.

while high above in the leggy, old-growth giant trees that line the banks, parrots, toucans, and a hundred other species of brightly coloured birds chatter constantly. Most of the privately owned boats that make the long run north are 5 to 6 metres (15 to 20 feet) in length, constructed of thin plywood or fiberglass, and powered by noisy outboard motors. Be prepared for a long boat ride during which you can't move around.

A few kilometres north of the tiny village of Pacuare, the Tortuguero Channels breach the southern boundary of **Tortuguero National Park.** Officially founded in 1970, the park today encompasses nearly 20,250 hectares (50,000 acres) of tropical lowland rain forest bounded on the east by wide, white beach. The latter, about 22 km (14 miles) in length, is the largest mating and nesting site in the entire Caribbean for green, hawksbill, and leatherback sea turtles.

Many other wild animals reside in Tortuguero as well. Howler and capuchin monkeys, three-toed sloths, and Central American tapirs are just some of the park's permanent, fairly-easy-to-spot (particularly along the channels) inhabitants. Tortuguero area residents say that a healthy population of jaguars—which are known locally as *el tigre*—also reside here. Tree climbers, water lovers, and the largest wild feline in the New World, these retiring creatures generally stay as far from human habitation as possible, however, and are seldom seen by man.

In the waterways themselves there are crocodiles, caiman, river otters, West Indian manatees, and a 2-

A green sea turtle lumbers ashore at Tortuguero to lay her eggs.

metre- (6½-foot-) long living fossil known as the gaspar fish, which has inhabited the region for more than 90 million years. Swimming in the Tortuguero Channels, by the way, is not a good idea. Sharks often enter the lagoons and rivers from the nearby Caribbean, and in the muddy waters have been known to attack bathers.

The Tortuguero rain forest is so dense and wet (the park averages about 500 cm, or 197 inches, of rain each year) that not even local guides go very far inland without good reason. If you wish to explore the park on your own, you can do so by renting a dugout canoe or by joining a guided nature walk, both of which are offered by most Tortuguero village lodges.

The village of **Tortuguero,** straddling a narrow strip of palm-shaded sand between Tortuguero Lagoon and the Caribbean, lies at the northernmost spur of Tortuguero National Park. A sleepy shantytown of some 300 people, it consists of perhaps three dozen wood-and-thatch houses, a park ranger station, a few tiny hotels, a disco, and a couple of small *tiendas* (shops). The wide, green Tortuguero Lagoon, on the western side of the village, is one of the prettiest segments of water along the Tortuguero Channels. Boat docks, canoe rentals, and the national-park ranger station are located on the lagoon shore near the center of town. A hundred metres to the east of the village lies

During egg-laying season, turtle tracks are a common sight on the protected sands of Tortuguero.

the Caribbean. The long, unbroken white-sand beach here is a great place to sunbathe and look for seashells, but locals recommend that you not venture very far out in the water. Large numbers of sharks and barracudas inhabit the area, and even village residents seldom swim in water more than waist deep.

From Tortuguero, you can return south by boat to Puerto Moín via the Tortuguero Channels, fly to San José, or continue north another 40 km (25 miles) through the **Barra del Colorado National Wildlife Refuge** to the Río Colorado and the tiny coastal village of Barra del Colorado. If you choose the last, you'll have to travel by boat, and unless you can convince a local fisherman to make the trip, transport will have to be arranged in advance through a travel agent or tour operator in San José. The two-hour boat ride from Tortuguero north to Barra del Colorado along the Tortuguero Channels through the wildlife refuge is extraordinarily scenic.

The village of **Barra del Colorado,** located about 1 km (½ mile) upstream from where the wide and murky Río Colorado empties into the Caribbean, is inhabited mostly by fishermen and their families. Outsiders come to Barra del Colorado for one reason only, to stay at Central America's most famous fishing resort, the Río Colorado Lodge. The first two cabins at the lodge were constructed in 1973; today this cosy compound built on stilts near the center of Barra del Colorado Sur has 18 spacious rooms, a complex of open-air dining rooms and breezy verandahs, its own zoo, and one of the best-equipped fleets of sport-fishing boats in the Caribbean. Some of the best tarpon and snook fishing in the world is found along Costa Rica's northern Caribbean coast, and most guests at the lodge are serious anglers.

From Barra del Colorado, the quickest and cheapest way to return to San José is by air (the strip is adjacent to Río

Colorado Lodge). Travelair, the domestic Costa Rican airline, offers daily flights from San José to both Barra del Colorado and Tortuguero.

THE PACIFIC COAST

If Costa Rica is an eco-tourist's dream come true, its Pacific coast provides a real-life fantasy world to accompany that dream. From Guanacaste just south of the Nicaraguan border to Corcovado just north of Panamá, much of the Pacific shore is protected land. Each of these national parks, biopreserves, and wildlife refuges has a personality of its own. They share enough wildlife in common, however, to have

Tarpon Fishing

A typical day at the Río Colorado Lodge begins at 5:00 AM when a monumental breakfast is served on the open-air verandah. Precisely an hour later the fleet of modern, 20-foot-long fishing boats—each carrying a professional guide and two anglers—leaves the dock and heads for the mouth of the Río Colorado, a five-minute boat ride to the east.

Of the two principal game fish found in the Barra del Colorado area, tarpon and snook, it is tarpon, a bony, torpedo-shaped creature weighing from 7½ to more than 37 kg (20 to 100 pounds) that is by far the more popular. From December through May these voracious fish migrate into the Río Colorado delta by the thousands to feed on shrimp and other small crustaceans, and at the peak of the season a single angler may hook as many as 30 or 40 tarpon a day. The real fun, however, is not in landing the fish (all tarpon caught here are released unharmed), but in the battle itself. When hooked, tarpon fling themselves from the water in a display of aerial acrobatics that no other game fish on earth comes close to matching.

you searching for one more glimpse of yesterday's great sighting while you scan the canopy overhead for today's possibilities.

Be prepared for an exciting—but rugged—experience in the national parks of the Pacific coast. You'll get wet and muddy, sweat your brains out, nurse scrapes, massage bumps, soothe bruises, then fall asleep so soundly your tired muscles will bless you for finally giving them some relief. You'll trek through rivers, slide down slopes, squat motionless under a bush and try to ignore the swarms of mosquitoes homing in on you. You may not even get close enough to get the photograph you want, but you'll carry the memories of these experiences with you for the rest of your life.

A vast array of flora and fauna and untrod beaches are the reward for the trip to hard-to-reach Corcovado.

Puntarenas

The port city of Puntarenas, due west of San José near the mouth of the Golfo de Nicoya, is the arbitrary dividing point between the northern and southern Pacific coast areas. To the south are the great rain-forest preserves. North is a more climatically diverse terrain that covers both rain- and dry- forest areas. Both demand a sense of adventure and a

At Carara, all paths lead into the habitat of an astonishing array of exotic birds and other wildlife.

suspension of your need for the sort of pampering found on other, more resort-oriented vacations.

This is not a region of interesting towns and cities. Puntarenas and, to the south, Quepos, the principal coast towns, are little more than jumping-off points to other areas. Puntarenas, located just inside the Golfo de Nicoya, is the principal port city on Costa Rica's western shore. About 100 km (62 miles) west of San José—all of it by major highway—the city is only about an hour-and-a-half drive and therefore easily accessible to Juan Santamaría International Airport as well.

A town of fewer than 40,000 citizens, Puntarenas grew as a cargo port during the 19th century, principally to launch locally grown coffee and bananas on their journeys to consumers east and west (the eastern voyage was a very long trip in the days before the Panamá Canal). With the development of Puerto Limón on the Caribbean coast during the latter half of this century, Puntarenas lost its trade with the east coast of North America and markets in Europe. Today, though touring vessels still dock at the port, the town seems little more than an embarkation point for visitors heading out on journeys of exploration into Costa Rica's Pacific-coast parks and reserves, or to the beaches that line the coast. The skinny peninsula that holds the town is as narrow as 100 metres (328 feet) at its thinnest and only six avenues across at its widest point. A spin about the town will reveal the typical Catholic church surrounded by a central plaza and the local market.

The Pacific Coast South of Puntarenas

Forty km (25 miles) southeast of Puntarenas along the paved coastal highway to Quepos lies **Carara Biological Reserve.** A few miles before reaching the reserve's entrance, stop at the Tárcoles bridge and study the edges of the river for any movement; what first appears to be a sandbar may well be the back of a caiman enjoying the sun. Iguanas are also plentiful here; look closely because one may well be resting on a limb just a few feet in front of you.

Carara is one of the beneficiaries of Costa Rica's position between North and South America; an abundance of wildlife flows into this transition zone between the continents. Rain forests like Carara, however, are also important to the health of the rest of the planet, supplying a significant percentage of the world's oxygen supply.

Trails here are numerous. Many are access roads for vehicles, but vehicular traffic is extremely limited, so trekkers can penetrate the forest along these wide paths without having to battle the underbrush. If the canopy begins to shudder and shake, you've probably been overtaken by a group of white-throated capuchins, who swing through the date trees, gobbling fruit and shaking the trees as they go. Things fall, and terrestrial animals follow along the ground, foraging. Wait quietly, and you might spot a peccary or an anteater crossing the trail.

Whenever it might please him, a capuchin monkey is sure to steal the show.

Keep an eye trained on the path for a parade of leaf-cutter ants carrying their green harvests. If you spot a line of them or a straggler or two, follow where they lead. One such trail may take you to a large ficus tree, where, along an entomological superhighway, the ants move—thousands of them—carrying thumbnail-size cuttings of leaf in one direction, returning in the opposite direction for another load. Their course is an engineering marvel. It includes land bridges over such obstacles as rutted rain gullies and tunnels beneath tree roots and other large obstacles.

Notice also the beautiful heliconias, hanging in clusters that appear like blood-drenched spearheads. Alighting here and there are brown-and-yellow heliconius butterflies, whose nine-month lifespan is the longest of any lepidopteran. Here too are red-billed hummingbirds, stopping to slurp nectar from a flower along their 19,200-km (12,000-mile) migratory route.

The town of **Quepos,** south of Carara and adjacent to Manuel Antonio National Park, was little more than a sleepy seacoast village until the 1970s. During the last two decades, however, tourists drawn to the beautiful local beaches have brought some new, much-needed revenue to the town. Nonetheless, it remains little more than a tiny village, here to support beach-goers, sport-fishermen, and the area's palm-oil plantations. There are actually five beaches in the area:

Espadilla, Espadilla Sur, Manuel Antonio, Puerto Escondido, and Playita. All are lovely and, if you have the time, a great place for a cool dip.

Manuel Antonio National Park is the tiny-but-mighty jewel in the national park system's crown. It is literally next door to Quepos; drive south on a nameless, numberless paved road for about 2 km (1½ miles) to the park's entrance.

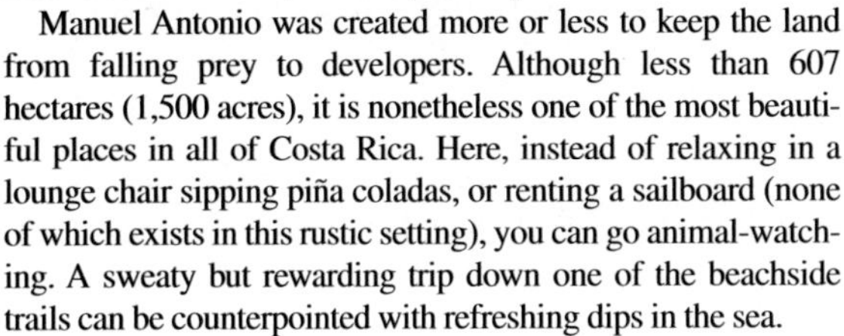

Manuel Antonio was created more or less to keep the land from falling prey to developers. Although less than 607 hectares (1,500 acres), it is nonetheless one of the most beautiful places in all of Costa Rica. Here, instead of relaxing in a lounge chair sipping piña coladas, or renting a sailboard (none of which exists in this rustic setting), you can go animal-watching. A sweaty but rewarding trip down one of the beachside trails can be counterpointed with refreshing dips in the sea.

What can you see in an area so small and so confined? If you're quiet, light-footed, and cautious, the answer is quite a lot. More than 100 species of mammals and nearly 200 types of birds have been recorded in the park. Chief among the sighting prizes is the squirrel monkey (one of the rarest of the New World primates), which, it is feared, is headed for extinction. Your odds are much better with the white-throated capuchins, groups of which travel through Manuel Antonio's treetops while earthbound peccaries, tapirs, and armadillos trail below.

A dozen islands that dot the waters offshore near Manuel Antonio are havens for gaggles of pelicans, boobies, and frigates, among other birds. An elaborate reef system has developed between the islands and the beach. Within a few dozen metres from the shore, you can wade, then dog paddle to the closest of these, which provide for a fair snorkeling experience.

There is no easy overland route south from Manuel Antonio to **Corcovado National Park.** Frankly, there is no easy land route to Corcovado, period. The coast road is un-

A shore-hugging cruise is an ideal—and relaxing—way to visit the national parks along the Pacific Coast.

paved from Quepos south to Palmar Norte (where you can pick up the Inter-American Highway), a distance of about 90 km (56 miles), with portions of it passable only in the dry season. You can also follow this unpaved road 67 km (41 miles) to Barú, then take the paved road northeast to San Isidro and get on the Inter-American Highway there, but that stretch of dirt road will take you hours and will be a nerve-racking journey in wet weather. The only other option is to circle back toward San José, pick up the Inter-American Highway 14 km (9 miles) east of Atenas, then take it south to the access route to Corcovado—but this is a trip of more than 500 km, or 300 miles!

The easiest and most pleasant way to visit Corcovado is from the sea, aboard one of the small motor vessels which now offer multi-day Pacific coast expeditions. The logistical headaches—getting to and into the park, then locating a place to bed down—are simply eliminated.

There are several things that make Corcovado National Park special. Its 40,500 hectares (100,000 acres) account for about one-third of the Península de Osa, which juts out into the Pacific just north of the Panamanian border and comprises perhaps the best example of Pacific coastal rain forest left in North America. Its incredibly diverse assemblage of flora and fauna offers one of the most rewarding opportunities for bird- and animal-watching concentrated in a single, well-defined area. It also includes a range of geography and variety of habitat that extends from lowland swamp, mangrove, and alluvial plain to mountain cloud forest, where the annual rainfall averages more than 500 cm (195 inches) per year.

Some 400 bird species (nearly half the species found in Costa Rica) have been seen here, along with 140 types of mammals and 120 kinds of amphibians and reptiles. Corcovado has only recently been disturbed by man. In the 1960s, loggers began to penetrate the park to harvest some of its many varieties of trees. Partly to put a stop to that, the area was declared a national park in 1975. Then gold was discovered in its streams, which brought an influx of miners during the 1980s. They were evicted in 1986, but not without hard feelings on both sides, and the two groups have been meeting to work out compromises ever since. For now, the miners stay on the periphery of the park, but long-term ecological solutions will require understanding the importance of the natural environment to a population that needs to earn a living.

Whatever method you use to penetrate Corcovado's wilderness, be extremely attentive along the hiking trails or you'll miss the less-obvious attractions—a sloth clinging to the underside of a tree limb, a giant blue morpho butterfly fluttering over a stream, a toucan gawking from the rain-forest canopy. Also be aware that the show here changes quickly. For while you are noting the relationship between the trees and their various clinging vines, you may miss the quick pass of a violaceous trogon, or a rare scarlet macaw (described as a red-crayon swipe across a patch of blue), or a giant harpy eagle.

Seventeen km (11 miles) west of the Península de Osa is **Isla del Caño,** a 304-hectare (750-acre) biological reserve. Access to the island requires a boat, but most coastal cruise expeditions stop here at least for the day. Caño Island is noted for its beautiful beaches and a pre-Columbian Indian graveyard dotted with giant spherical stones. Most of the island's hiking trails lead past these mysterious spheres. Archaeologists have thus far failed to come up with conclusive explanations for either what purpose the stones served or who made them.

The short hike up the sides of a mesa from the beach affords dramatic views of the surrounding sea. And beneath the glass-clear, lusciously warm waters lives a rich assortment of sealife. A half-dozen reefs harbour more than a dozen species of coral and colonies of inhabitants that range from nearly microscopic fish to giant rays, an assortment of sea turtles, and even an occasional passing pod of whales.

The island's beaches are silk-smooth light brown sand, with charcoal swipes of black that change length and direction with each receding wave. Jetties and piles of black rock mark off the beaches and act as natural breakwaters for the riptide. Tiny rivulets empty fresh water from the morning rain on the plateau into the sea, providing miniature feeding estuaries for stiff-legged seabirds. A beach here is a lovely place to park for a day, haul out the picnic baskets and a cold beer or a chilled bottle of white wine, and get a touch of sun.

The Pacific Coast North of Puntarenas

Most of the principal wildlife areas in the coastal region north of Puntarenas can be explored on a day trip or a longer excursion, depending upon your interest in the local flora and fauna. Suffice it to say that the longer you stay the more you are likely to see. To maximize the effectiveness of your journeys into the wilds here, local guides are important. They know the effects of season, changes in weather and terrain, time of day, and method of approach. Making arrangements for a guide in advance of your trip is a good idea.

Cruising the Coast

In many respects, the seaborne method is the best way to visit many of Costa Rica's Pacific-coast parks, Corcovado among them. Various expedition and cruise companies offer multi-day excursions, but one of the best is a Costa Rican-owned company called Temptress Cruises. Voyages embark from Puntarenas and cover the coast from Bahía Santa Elena (Santa Elena Bay) near the Nicaraguan border to Corcovado, down toward the Panamanian border.

Accommodations aboard the 60-passenger Temptress are a bit tight but quite comfortable. All cabins are air-conditioned and include two single bunks, a sink, and a shower. The dining salon serves breakfast and dinner, and lunches are either packed for hikes ashore or served on the beach at midday. The alfresco bar on the top deck aft, a great place for a tall, cool one in the late afternoon, is also the gathering place for after-dinner activities. Folkloric troupes are brought aboard periodically to entertain. The crew is efficient and personable, and most members speak English as well as Spanish. Tours are conducted by university-trained naturalists who are knowledgeable in the great biodiversity of their country. All sightseeing and exploration travel to and from the ship is aboard motorized Zodiac rafts.

Southern cruises generally run from November to May. From June through October, cruises alternate between north and south; therefore, you can then chose either itinerary, or arrange a back-to-back trip to do the entire coast.

Spherical stones like these, perfectly round but carved without metal tools, remain a mystery to this day.

The rough, gravel access road to the **Monteverde Cloud Forest Preserve** is off the Inter-American Highway, about 33 km (20 miles) north of Puntarenas. Locals will tell you that you can make it in an ordinary vehicle in dry weather but you will need four-wheel drive when it rains. It's a teeth-rattling, spine-jarring trip that requires about two-and-a-half hours from Puntarenas in good weather.

The end of the road will deposit you at the Monteverde information center and gift shop, where you can make arrangements for a guide if you want one. Then you'll have the privilege of sinking calf-deep into muddy ooze, sliding down slick clay slopes, and parading through the low-hung clouds until your clothes feel as if they are mouldering before your eyes. This is a cloud forest. In a cloud forest, it's not rain you're feeling but literally the undersides of clouds resting directly on the hilltops. Here there's a whole different world of flora and fauna—plants and animals that thrive in the always damp, sometimes chilly landscape above the cloud line.

The prize sighting in Monteverde is the quetzal, a bird of striking colour and shape. Its golden beak protrudes from a green-hooded head that tops a red breast. The V formed by the split tail feathers—grey-black on top, white underneath—gives the appearance of a silk-lined tuxedo jacket. The quetzal is endangered because of its ever-shrinking habitat and the increasing predatory strikes of weasels and snakes that like to dine on its eggs.

A shy bird, the quetzal will have you hoofing off the trail, across fields, over fences, then craning your neck and straining your eyes just for a glimpse, unable to give up after hours of anticipation. When you do finally spot one, high in the canopy pecking at the fruit of a wild avocado, the sense of accomplishment is unforgettable.

The most popular trail in Monteverde is the **Sendero Bosque Nuboso,** a 4-km (2½-mile) round trip interpretive stroll to the Continental Divide. Just outside the entrance to the preserve, stop in at the Hummingbird Gallery. Feeders hanging from trees here attract nearly a dozen different species of rain-forest hummingbirds; most can be approached and photographed with ease.

Monteverde has grown larger over the past several years and has even spawned a kind of satellite preserve called **El Bosque Eterno de los Niños,** also known as the First International Children's Rain Forest. The idea for the Children's Rain Forest originated with a group of schoolchildren in Sweden who decided to do what they could to help save the tropical rain forests. They raised money—through recycling projects, bake sales, and contributions—to buy 6 hectares (15 acres) to be set aside as a wildlife preserve. Within five years El Bosque's protected lands, adjacent to the eastern borders of the Monteverde preserve, had grown to almost 20,250 hectares (50,000 acres).

Some of the widest variations in Costa Rica's extensive biological diversity are found in the **Palo Verde National Park,** which now also includes the Dr. Rafael Lucas Rodríguez Caballero National Wildlife Refuge. The park is due west of Monteverde and northwest of Puntarenas. It sits in the lowlands along the northern shoreline of the Río Tempisque, west of the Río Bebedero and just above the confluence of both rivers, where they empty into the Golfo de Nicoya. Here the terrain varies from marsh, grassland, and savannah to dry forest.

Palo Verde, like many of the national parks and preserves along the Pacific coast, is not easily reached by land. The access road is south off the Inter-American Highway at Bagaces, about 20 km (12½ miles) north of Cañas and 90 km (55 miles) northwest of Puntarenas; it runs south another 20 km (12½ miles) to the park. Constructed primarily of dirt and gravel, it is wet and muddy during the rainy season and very dusty during the dry season. It's about a two-hour drive from Bagaces to the park. Most coastal cruise expeditions call here as part of their northern itinerary.

The trees wear a thick covering of green during the summer wet season, then thin noticeably during the dry season (December to April), which allows for much easier animal-watching. In the dry months, watering holes and small ponds also shrink or dry up, which in turn adds to the concentration of wildlife around the remaining sources of water, again affording wonderful observation points. In the dry season the mosquitoes, gnats, and other flying pests that swarm the area during the rainy periods are far less concentrated, driven off by the stiff winds that are prevalent during that time of the year.

Palo Verde has the usual Costa Rican complement of mammals, reptiles, butterflies, and other colourful insects, but the big attraction here is its great diversity of birds—a combination of the year-round residential community and migratory waterfowl. Some 275 species have been recorded, but it is not so much the number of species that is appealing here—there are more species in other areas—as it is the unusual variety. Among the residents or regular transients, for example, is the jabiru stork, a magnificent creature said to be the largest stork in the world. Its colouring is predominantly white with a grey-hooded head, set off by a blood-red neckband. Only a handful of jabirus nest here, but the other, more common varieties of birds you might see—among them wrens, hummingbirds, ospreys, caracaras, and a great collection of wading birds—will make the trip worthwhile.

Scenes like this reward hikers in Monteverde Cloud Forest.

It is a tribute to Costa Rica's long-standing aversion to military strongmen that the country's national hero is not a conquistador, general, or warlord, but a young *campesino,* Juan Santamaría. Santamaría's moment of glory came in early 1856, when he was part of an all-volunteer army assembled to drive back American adventurer William Walker, who had designs on controlling most of Central America and enslaving a good deal of the population. After routing the forces of Nicaragua, Walker pushed south into Costa Rica and dug in at a hacienda called Casona Santa Rosa in the northwestern part of the country. Here, 9,000 Costa Rican volunteers met and defeated the band of mercenary raiders, driving them back into Nicaragua. Pursued by the Costa Ricans, Walker sought shelter in a fort at the town of Rivas. Santamaría volunteered to torch the wooden fort there and was killed in the battle.

Almost 48,600 hectares (120,000 acres) around the hacienda where the Costa Ricans met and defeated William Walker were set aside to commemorate the event, and in 1971 were declared the **Santa Rosa National Park.** The hacienda where the famous battle took place, familiarly called La Casona, has been restored to its 19th-century character. A museum has also been installed in portions of the hacienda and its adjoining and adjacent buildings.

The main entrance to Santa Rosa is off the Inter-American Highway about 35 km (22 miles) north of the town of Liberia (Liberia, capital of Guanacaste province, is a town of fewer than 30,000 people, with little of interest to visitors), and about 155 km (96 miles) from Puntarenas. The easiest access to the park, however, is from the sea. Many coastal cruise expeditions stop here for a day as part of their northern itinerary.

Perhaps unanticipated at the time by the park's founders (whose goal was to preserve the area's historical tradition) was Santa Rosa's significance as one of the largest examples of tropical dry forest in the Western Hemisphere. And this may be the most important legacy. The park comprises virtually all of the Península de Santa Elena and will help assure its maintenance as a natural forest and wildlife preserve.

Plant life that distinguishes dry forest from rain forest lines the trails here. A common tree here is the guanacaste, namesake of the province and the national tree of Costa Rica. The maroon-red trunk of the gumbo-limbo, or naked Indian tree, is another common sight. Endangered cedars and giant ashes spread their crowns to the more abundant light in these thinner forests. Tree-dwelling vines and other plants here are also representative of the climatic conditions; cacti of all kinds, for example, grow in abundance.

In the air and trees above the trails, you're apt to see many of the 250 species of birds that have been identified here, including violaceous trogons, crested guan, and long-tailed manakins. There's no paucity of mammal life here either, with more than 100 species identified; among the most common are coatimundis, peccaries, tapirs, and white-tailed deer.

The stars of nature's circus in this corner of the world are the reptiles, however. A scaly grey iguana resting on a tree limb (or an immature green one sunning in a patch of light) may arouse your interest. Santa Rosa is one of the few remaining nesting places for the olive ridley turtle. While these sea creatures are in the area from August through December, it is during September and October that their activity along the sandy beaches is most concentrated. Ask the rangers at the administration center to point you in the right direction.

Carry plenty of Costa Rican money in small denominations outside of San José.

Unlike most of the other nature refuges along the Pacific coast, **Tamarindo National Wildlife Refuge** on the western shore of the huge Nicoya Peninsula requires at least a two-day visit. To get here from Puntarenas, travel 120 km (74 miles) north on the Inter-American Highway to Liberia, then 20 km (12 miles) west on route 21 to Guardia, where the road turns south and in another 25 km (15 miles) narrows to a secondary road just south of Filadelfia. At Belén the road forks. Take the right, or west, fork and follow the signs for another 35 km (22 miles) through the tiny villages of Cartagena, Portegolpe, Huacas, and Villarreal, until you get to the village of Tamarindo. The coastline is about a 1-km (½-mile) hike from Tamarindo village. Just about anyone in town can point you to the trail.

It is a relatively tiny piece of real estate (405 hectares/1,000 acres), but along the wide beaches here giant leatherback turtles come ashore to nest from October through March. These largest of sea turtles grow to 1½ metres (5 feet) in length and can weigh more than 258 kgs (800 pounds). They are distinguishable from other sea turtles not only by their great size but by their green-black leathery backs, as opposed to the distinctive hard shell of other sea turtles.

During nesting season as many as 200 females a night have been observed waddling ashore at Playa Grande, paddling up the beach to where they deposit up to 100 eggs apiece, each the approximate size, shape, and colour of a ping-pong ball. It's difficult to see the nesting process without disturbing the environment, which may be why the wildlife refuge does not even appear on the official map of the Costa Rican Tourist Board. Perhaps the best way to observe any portion of the nesting ritual is from a boat. Local boat operators will take you offshore for a fee, which varies widely but can be negotiated.

The west coast of the Península de Nicoya is not just for turtle nesting, however. From Playa Panamá in the north near Guardia to Playa Santa Teresa near the southern tip of the peninsula, the shoreline stretches about 200 km (124 miles), much of it beautiful beaches. An all-weather gravel road runs along the coast, connecting Tamarindo to Playa Santa Teresa, a dis-

White-tailed deer and 100 other kinds of fauna roam Santa Rosa National Park.

tance of about 150 km (93 miles). The beach fronts vary in type from thickly forested to wide stretches of sand that range in colour from beige to coffee. Most are lightly populated, even in the busy dry months.

NORTH-CENTRAL COSTA RICA

The north-central portion of Costa Rica has been little affected by the 20th century. Only a small percentage of Costa Rica's three million inhabitants reside in this corrugated landscape. Undisturbed for the most part by logging or other destructive human endeavours, this land of pristine lowland forests and smouldering volcanoes is a mosaic of scenic terrain that will astonish even the most veteran travellers with its incredible beauty.

The Road to Arenal

The principal route for visitors in this part of Costa Rica is the Naranjo–Quesada–Arenal road, which at Naranjo turns right off the Inter-American Highway west-northwest of San José and runs in a northwesterly direction. The 44-km (27-mile) segment of the Inter-American road from San José to Naranjo and the beginning of the Arenal is an easily navigable, well-kept four-lane route. It begins in downtown San José as Avenida Central, becomes Paseo Colón as it travels west, then leaves the city in a northerly direction as Calle 42.

Climbing slightly upward into the foothills of the Cordillera Central (Central Highlands), the highway carries motorists through an open, scenic landscape dotted with cattle ranches, ornamental nurseries, small truck farms, and sprawling coffee plantations. The turnoff to the village of Naranjo and the Naranjo–Quesada–Arenal road is 4 km (2½ miles) beyond the government-operated highway toll booth. Well-marked by signs, the junction is on the right.

Perched atop a ridge in the verdant foothills a five-minute drive beyond the turnoff, **Naranjo** is a low-slung, bustling agricultural town that holds little of interest for visitors except for a beautiful cathedral built in 1924.

The distance from Naranjo north to the village of Zarcero is about 21 km (13 miles). On a clear day views from the road of the Central Valley to the west and the sprawling hillside coffee plantations below are spectacular. For much of the distance the road is lined with living ornamental fences—colourful, manicured bushes (most of them formed from a plant called Indian cane), which keep cattle in their pastures and block the wind.

The charming village of **Zarcero,** with its narrow, winding streets, cosy, tile-roofed homes, and small but attractive church, is nestled in the foothills of the Cordillera Central, which divides the Central Valley on the west from the San Carlos plain on the northeast. Zarcero's famous **topiary gardens,** located in the main square in front of the church, can be easily seen on the right as you drive through the village on the main road headed north.

The fairly large agricultural hub of Ciudad Quesada, 28 km (17 miles) north of Zarcero, is known for its delicious white cheese, as is Zarcero. Five minutes north of Ciudad Quesada, just where the road makes a sharp turn to the left, the lava-blackened cinder cone of Arenal Volcano—usually spouting a spiral of steam and gas—comes into view on the right. There's a small roadside parking area here.

At the stop sign in Florencia, 8 km (5 miles) northwest of Ciudad Quesada, you can go straight to reach Arenal Volcano if you wish, but to stay on the Naranjo–Quesada–Arenal road (which is straighter and in better shape), turn right at the stop sign and go toward the village of Muelle. Eleven kilometres (7 miles) farther north, just before you reach Muelle, you'll come to the junction of Route 4 on the left, one of the few properly marked highways in Costa Rica. This is an important junction, so don't miss it. A left turn onto route 4 will take you to La Fortuna village and waterfall, Balneario Tabacón, Arenal Volcano, and Arenal Lake. If you want to visit Caño Negro National Wildlife Refuge, however (see page 83), instead of turning left on Route 4, drive straight through Muelle and follow the Muelle-Los Chiles road north to Los Chiles, about 74 km (46 miles).

West on route 4 out of Muelle, it's about 30 km (18 miles) to the small mountain village of **La Fortuna,** the nearest community to Arenal Volcano. La Fortuna's famous *catarata* (waterfall) is in a canyon about 5 km (3 miles) south of the village. If you're afraid of heights, don't go too near the edge at the falls' overlook; below, the hillside drops away steeply to a heavily forested valley floor, perhaps 150 metres (500 feet) below. Directly opposite and surrounded by pristine rain forest is the *catarata,* a stunning 75-meter- (246-foot-)

Not all nature's splendours are wild—vegetation is tamed into bizarre formations in the gardens of Zarcero's church.

high cascade of Río Fortuna water spewing out of a narrow cut in the mountainside.

West out of La Fortuna toward Arenal Volcano the road meanders through segments of farm-dotted rain forest as it climbs onto the shoulders of the cinder cone. About 5 km (3 miles) past the village limits, watch for a sign on the left that points to Los Lagos y Jungla Senderos (The Lakes and Jungle Trails). Set in a valley at the end of the road just below Arenal volcano's eastern flank, **Los Lagos** is like a jewel in the jungle. About 1 hectare (3 acres) in size and surrounded by primary (uncut) rain forest, this emerald-green freshwater lagoon is one of the area's prettiest sights. Along the lake's shallow southern shore there are thatched picnic shelters, a tiny boat dock, and a concrete ramp from which swimmers can enter the water without getting their feet muddy.

In the forest surrounding the lake, brightly coloured jungle birds glide from tree to tree like flying rainbows, and troops of howler monkeys often wander down off the volcano's slopes to feed. In addition to monkeys, visitors may also spot other rainforest animals, among them pacas, deer, and tapirs. There are four *senderos* (trails) here, the beginning of each marked by a small sign. Three of the trails are less than a kilometre (½ mile) in length and lead to different observation points above the lagoon. A longer trail, about 5 km (3 miles) in length, meanders west through the rain forest to another lagoon farther up the valley. The entry fee to Los Lagos is less than a dollar, paid to either the farmer who runs the place or whichever of his children happens to be near the gate shack when you arrive.

Balneario Tabacón (Tabacón Hot Springs) is a concentration of beautiful steaming pools and waterfalls about five minutes west of Los Lagos on the main road from La Fortuna to Arenal Lake. The bathhouse complex is adjacent to the highway on the left (west). "Spring" is a misnomer in this case. The water is actually a thermal river that flows from the magma-filled bowels of Arenal Volcano just upstream. A lovely, tile-roofed Spanish-style villa here, surrounded by fountains, pools, a water slide, and extensive, exquisitely manicured gardens, has both lounging and changing rooms. From most of the pools, bathers can see the huge cone of the volcano only a few kilometres (one mile or so) to the southeast.

Grumbles, groans, and roars continue to greet visitors to Arenal Volcano, which blew its top two decades ago.

Arenal Volcano

Arenal Volcano, elevation 1,633 metres (5,358 feet), blew its top for the first time in recorded history in July 1968, blanketing vast terrain (and one small village) with hot ash and lava, and killing 78 people. Most local residents were not aware that Arenal was a volcano, and no one suspected the mountain was alive and dangerous until it was far too late.

The rough road to the only "official" volcano-viewing area turns off the La Fortuna–Arenal Lake highway about 15 km (9 miles) west of La Fortuna. The junction, marked by a "Parqueo and Arenal Observatory Lodge" sign, is on the left. The official *parqueo* (parking lot) is on the volcano's lower slopes about 3 km (2 miles) from the junction.

From the parking lot, visitors are welcome to hike up the lower shoulders of the mountain for a closer look at the steaming fumaroles. Unlike Poás and Irazú volcanoes to the southeast, however, Arenal is clearly healthy, and is quite dangerous. New vents are opening constantly on the mountainside (usually with no warning), spewing poisonous gases into the air and spilling rivers of red-hot magma down the slopes. If you hike, don't go more than a few hundred feet from the parking lot. Several people are killed each year on Arenal, most of them tourists foolishly attempting to climb to the top.

Views of the mountain are magnificent anytime, but visiting the volcano at night—when bright, narrow streams of crimson magma can be seen cascading down the mountain

Three-Toed Sloths

If you've never seen a three-toed sloth (known as the three-fingered sloth in some parts of Central America), you probably will in Caño Negro. Small and clothed in a dense, shaggy mat of mossy-looking hair, this docile, sluggish, tailless mammal is one of nature's most interesting creatures. Its overall colour is normally silvery-grey and its face—a wide-eyed mask covered with short hair—is white or cream-coloured. Strangely enough, its fur is often infested with swarms of moths, which scuttle in and out of the dense hair like fleas. Basically tree animals, sloths spend most of their lives nibbling on fruit while hanging from the limbs or trunks of towering jungle trees such as the papaw or guarumo. According to scientists, they leave their feeding tree only about once a month, at night, to defecate.

Another animal commonly seen in Caño Negro is the paca, a large rodent that resembles a bug-eyed rat. Night animals (the best time to see them is at dawn or dusk), pacas spend much of their time feeding on jungle fruits that have fallen to the forest floor. Though shy and retiring, they are nasty fighters when cornered, chewing away at their attackers with long, sharp front teeth.

and the clouds above the caldera turn bright-orange from the superheated lava—is an unforgettable experience. The Arenal Lake road is dangerous at night for motorists unaccustomed to local driving habits, however, so if possible arrange to take a guided excursion from your hotel.

A few kilometres west of the volcano is **Arenal Lake,** a huge, multi-armed reservoir created in 1979 to provide hydro-electric power for San José and other Costa Rican cities. Today, covering some 130 square km (50 square miles) and filled with a species of humpbacked, brightly coloured game fish known as rainbow bass, it is one of Central America's best-known fishing lakes. Because of the 20- to 30-knot winds that sweep across the northwest end of the lake from December through March, Arenal has also become one of the most popular sailboarding lakes in the Western Hemisphere. Windsurfing experts say there is simply no other inland body of water like it anywhere.

Caño Negro Wildlife Refuge

Located almost on the Nicaraguan border, Caño Negro Wildlife Refuge is best viewed from a *panga* (covered canoe), hireable, with guide and for a modest fee, in the village of Caño Negro on the Río Frío. If you're not on an organized tour, head north from Muelle to the town of Los Chiles, about 74 km (46 miles). From Los Chiles, turn southwest on the road to Caño Negro village and drive another 23 km (14 miles).

Of all Costa Rica's nature preserves, Caño Negro probably has the largest viewable selection of indigenous wildlife. Among the larger animals commonly seen by visitors are crocodiles, tapirs, monkeys, river otters, white-tailed deer, peccaries, anteaters, and sloths. Jaguars and cougars also reside here, as do a number of species of rare butterflies and more than 200 kinds of birds.

WHAT TO DO

SPORTS

Diving and Snorkeling

With more than 20 major dive sites (many in the Gulf of Papagayo), the northwest Pacific coast of Costa Rica on the Nicoya Peninsula offers scuba diving in a magnificent setting throughout the year. Visibility isn't great—6 to 12 metres (20 to 40 feet depending upon the severity of the algae blooms), but the water is warm and the underwater scenery is grand. Huge schools of fish are the norm; divers will usually see jacks, moray eels, sharks, eagle rays, puffers, and countless species of brightly coloured reef fish. The inshore waters also boast some fantastic underwater rock formations and even a few wrecks.

Caño Island, off the southwest coast, is known for beautiful coral reefs and winding undersea canyons. Coco Island, touted by Jacques Cousteau as one of the finest deep-water dive sites in the world, is also popular. Both require boat access (call Temptress Cruises, (506) 232-6672 in Costa Rica, or Aggressor Fleet, 504-385-2628 in the U.S., for information).

The best diving on the Caribbean coast is on the reefs near Cahuita National Park, and near Punta Uva south of Puerto Viejo near the Panamá border. Non-certified divers on both coasts can take lessons from local licenced instructors. A full range of first-class equipment is available for rent.

Hiking and Backpacking

Costa Rica's national parks are ideal for trekking, though you'll need a guide for ventures away from well-marked trails. All of the country's national parks and most wildlife reserves maintain a network of hiking and nature trails.

Caño Island, surrounded by glorious underwater flora and fauna, is one of the some 20 major dive sites in Costa Rica.

Overnight or multi-night treks—such as an organized ascent of Mount Chirripó, Costa Rica's highest peak—can be arranged through local outfitters. (Contact Jungle Trails, (506) 255-3486 for more information.)

Mountain Biking

With its mountainous terrain and thousands of miles of forest trails, Costa Rica is the ideal spot for mountain biking. Several companies based in San José offer both organized day trips and extended biking vacations (see page 107). Highway biking is not recommend because of traffic and a lack of bike lanes.

Sea Kayaking

Ocean kayaking is rapidly gaining devotees in Costa Rica, mainly because almost anyone can do it after only a lesson or two. Besides being a great way to tour the coast, kayaks also permit sea access to slow-moving jungle rivers where other boats can't go (and where wildlife is less timid). Presently, most sea kayaking takes place on the Pacific coast. Rentals are available at a number of upscale resorts.

Sportfishing

Costa Rica's rich marine habitat also means excellent sportfishing. Along the Pacific coast—from the Gulf of Papagayo all the way to Golfito—anglers find some of the best bluewater and inshore fishing in the world (annual catch-and-release billfish tournaments usually raise record numbers of sailfish and marlin). Other common game fish are roosterfish, mahimahi, yellowfin tuna, grouper, and wahoo.

The Tortuguero Channels and the area around Barra del Colorado, on the northern Caribbean coast, have long been famous for fighting tarpon and snook; see pages 59 and 60 (box) Lake Arenal, the windsurfing center of Costa Rica, is also the place to catch an unusual species of gamefish: rainbow bass. Both areas have lodges that cater especially for fishermen.

Surfing

Many surf magazines have targeted Costa Rica as a world surfing hot spot. The almost constant, manageable wave action here means no lengthy waits between rides.

Puerto Viejo on the Caribbean side of the country has become known as a surfing center, as have Quepos and Jacó on the central Pacific coast. In all three towns you'll find shops that specialise in surfing equipment. Several hotels and resorts also have surfboard rentals; some even offer four-wheel-drive access to the more remote beaches.

Whitewater Rafting

Rafting on Costa Rica's wild and scenic rivers is perhaps the single most popular adventure sport in the country. Expert outfitters and river guides, using internationally approved equipment, escort thousands of whitewater adventurers down the Reventazón, Pacaure, Pascua, Corobicí, and Sarapiquí rivers every year.

Levels of difficulty range from a gentle float trip on the Río Corobicí near Cannas in the Guanacaste, to Class V wild-and-woolly adventures on the Pascua and Sarapiquí adjacent to Braulio Carrillo National Park. The Class III and IV Reventazón and Pacuare rivers, both in the Turrialba region, are the most popular with visitors. The tricky Pascua and Sarapiquí rivers usually attract more experienced rafters, while a trip down the Río Corobicí is an excellent trip for families or for birdwatchers.

Costa Rica's rivers are best for whitewater action from May to November, when they are swollen by runoff. Overnight and multi-day trips are available on most rivers. Excursions usually leave from San José; transportation, life jackets, and helmets are provided by the outfitter. For more information contact Costa Rica White Water, (506) 257-0766, Ríos Tropicales, (506) 233-6455, or Aventuras Naturales, (506) 225-3939.

Windsurfing

Experts have called Lake Arenal, Costa Rica's largest inland body of water, one of the world's top five windsurfing spots. From December to April breezes averaging 32 km/hr (20 miles an hour) blow steadily across the lake, carrying board sailors up and down Arenal's 42-km (26-mile) length. Several lodges on the west end of the lake offer windsurfing packages; see Hotel Tilawa in the Recommended Hotels section. The use of a sailboard is usually included in the price. For ocean sailboarding, check out Puerto Soley, on the northern Pacific coast.

Costa Rica's Beaches
Caribbean Coast

Puerto Limón–Cahuita Road. The Caribbean and its pure-white beach on one side, a dense tropical forest on the other. Swim, sunbathe, and beachcomb anywhere you can reach the water along the 47-km (29-mile) stretch.

Cahuita village. Excellent surfing and snorkeling conditions, a glass-bottomed-boat concession, and a pleasant, if cluttered (with drift logs) beach. Within walking distance of the Park.

Cahuita National Park. Wide, white beaches prettier than those of Cahuita village; snorkeling over the reef is superb. Nature trails bisect the beachside forest.

Puerto Viejo area. Snorkeling and surfing. The most popular beach is a long, beautiful stretch of black sand a ten-minute stroll from the village.

Punta Uva. The long, clean, palm-lined beaches in this tiny village are probably the prettiest on the Costa Rican Caribbean. At the rocky point of Punta Uva itself, superb reef snorkeling.

Tortuguero village. The long, unbroken white-sand beach here is a great place to sunbathe and look for seashells, but because of sharks the waters are not safe for swimming.

Pacific Coast

Quepos. There are five beautiful beaches in the area, very popular with visitors.

Isla del Caño. In a biological reserve noted for its beautiful beaches and a pre-Columbian Indian graveyard dotted with giant spherical stones, the beaches are silk-smooth light-brown sand. Glass-clear, lusciously warm waters with a rich assortment of sea life harboured by a half dozen reefs. (Access to the island is only by boat.)

West coast of PenÍnsula de Nicoya. The shoreline stretches about 200 km (124 miles), much of it beautiful beaches. Beach-fronts vary from thickly forested to wide stretches of sand that range in colour from beige to coffee. Most are lightly populated, even in high season.

Other Sports

Horseback riding in Costa Rica can give you easy access to remote beaches, isolated forest trails, and seldom-visited mountain ridges. Many lodges and resorts, especially those in Guanacaste and along the Pacific coast, offer horse rentals, riding lessons, and guides as part of their services.

Hot-air ballooning is also gaining popularity. It's a great way to view the forest canopy without confronting bugs and other jungle critters. So-called **canopy tours,** visits to the thick upper branches of towering rain-forest trees, are becoming very popular in Costa Rica. You can be winched up a giant tree to a platform where you'll perch for a few hours studying the wildlife (contact Serendipity Adventures, (506) 450-0328), or you can take a more comfortable 90-minute ride on a five-person gondola through the treetops (Aerial Tram, (506) 257-5961).

More adventuresome souls can sign up for **bungee jumping,** a new and popular sport in Costa Rica. For about $45, you can leap off an 81-metre- (265-foot-) high bridge, bounce and dangle for a while, then drop into the water for a swim to shore. For information, contact Tropical Bungee, tel. (506) 235-6455.

SHOPPING

Where to Shop and What to Buy

For the most part, shopping in Costa Rica is limited to San José and the Central Valley, especially if you're in the market for traditional arts and crafts. The country doesn't have an artistic heritage such as Guatemala or Mexico, but in recent years it has been working hard to establish a tradition of craftsmanship in wood, folkloric pieces, and leather.

Downtown San José

Outstanding work sometimes can be discovered among the booths at the Plaza de la Cultura, such as that of Poás-based Javier Aguero, who creates small, hand-painted clay wall masks using natural earth colours and feathers. These will soon be highly collectible, say experts, and prices will skyrocket.

Hammocks, long a Costa Rican legacy, can also be found in the Plaza. Of good quality (generally better than Mexican hammocks) and often made in Cartago, they are bartered as well as sold here in the Plaza. The vendors, usually relatives or friends of the hammock makers, are sharp dealers; they quote high and end low, so patience on the part of the buyer is a necessity. A hammock that will hold two people should cost about U.S. $25, though prices can drop a bit at the end of the day.

You're welcome. - *De nada.* (day nahdah)

Two other good buys here are colourful dangling earrings that you won't find north of the border, and simple women's sandals with a Guatemalan-style strap and leather soles that are great for tramping about the country.

The **Mercado Central** (don't carry anything that a pickpocket can reach) is usually crowded with shoppers. Mounds of fruits and vegetables are neatly displayed, alongside taco and sandwich stalls. Typical goods are cut flowers, leather goods, and clothing for the family. The market is between Avenida Central and Avenida 1, west of the Central Bank between Calles 6 and 8.

The **Mercado Nacional de Artesanía,** a large brown-stucco building behind the 1909 La Soledad church on Calle 11 and Avenida 2, was one of the first public markets to organize and display quality Costa Rican handicrafts under one roof. Don't be deterred by the shelves of tacky tourist teasers; look for featured crafts from various parts of the

At San José's Mercado Central the endless mounds of fresh tropical fruits catch the eye and whet the appetite.

country, such as splendid baskets, butterflies, and flowers made from tightly woven fiber or rope by Grupo Palmital, an association of talented women from Cartago. Inlaid table bowls and silver earrings are also notable here.

Raba, on Calle 11 not far from the Museo Nacional de Costa Rica, a half block south of Avenida Central, is a highbrow leather store dealing in finely crafted briefcases, women's purses lined with soft pigskin, and elaborate desk sets. Custom orders are a speciality. The family-owned business opened its doors in 1966, and has been at the same location for 15 years.

The **Boutique Annemarie,** in the Hotel Don Carlos, between Avenidas 7 and 9 on Calle 9, is recognized city-wide as a shopping mecca. The store is crammed with more than 4,000 items, including works from 600 craftspeople who sell direct to the boutique. Veteran shoppers say the key to Annemarie is to take your time and sort through the shelf clutter. Highly polished, museum-quality toucans carved from indigenous wood are good buys, as are jade necklaces and hand-painted pottery. Also on display is a large collection of fine art by Costa Rican artists, a wall of colourful and unusu-

Sarchí is famous for the brightly painted oxcarts its artisans produce.

al masks, and more jewellery and belts than you might ever want to see. If you don't spot the particular item you're looking for, an employee may be able to locate it.

El Pueblo

Alba Art Gallery in Centro Comercial El Pueblo is bulging with Costa Rican, Central American, and South American fine art. A major art dealer, director Mustehsan Farooqi has collected works by Francisco Amighetti (oils, drawings, and woodblocks) and Rafael Fernández (oils, pastels, and serigraphs). The gallery also has pieces by Marina Silva and Fernando Carballo.

On the upper level of El Pueblo is Del Río, another upmarket leather shop, similar to Raba, which sells top-grade Costa Rican handmade purses and men's luggage. Raba has a local factory and eight stores in the area.

Los Yoses

In the Los Yoses neighbourhood (east of downtown via Avenida Central, 200 metres/600 feet west of the Fuente de la Hispanidad fountain), **Galerías Casa Alameda** will satisfy shoppers who are close to the cutting edge of art and fashion. **Casa Alameda** is a small, elegant enclave of fashion, fine art, and import boutiques in a Beverly Hills mall-like setting.

Stefanel sells Italian-chic designer clothing. **Villa del Este** displays serving platters and bowls of high-quality

Mexican silver, decorative Peruvian silver, fine Mexican glassware, pewter pieces, Turkish rugs, and some Italian antique furniture. The clerks here are courteous and helpful.

A few steps across the interior patio, **Galería Real** features works from the best-known Costa Rican artists, sold with or without a frame (for collectors' convenience the gallery ships DHL). At the rear of the complex is the flashy **Vogue Boutique,** offering European designer fashions for women.

Café Ruiseñor, a sidewalk pastry shop at the entrance of Galerías Casa Alameda, is the perfect shopping finisher.

Moravia

North of downtown in Moravia, a suburb of San José located past the Guadalupe district on the road to San Jerónimo, twenty or so stores offering Central American crafts line Calle Las Artesanías. The time to shop here is after 10:00 A.M., when city traffic subsides. Focused browsers who dig around a bit may find unusual ceramic wind chimes, gorgeous Peruvian hand-painted wall mirrors, Guatemalan potholders, and decorative plates.

Signs:
rebajas **- sale**

In **Bri Bri,** an arts-and-crafts store that features the work of a Costa Rican Indian tribe, check out the dolls, the showy, one-of-a-kind handmade jewellery, and the excellent pre-Columbian reproduction figurines, masks, and candleholders.

Two doors down, **Malety** sells genuine Costa Rican leather at competitive prices. Small wallets for women, men's cowhide belts, attaché cases, sports bags, and a hundred other original items are available. Custom orders are encouraged.

Escazú

Another studio working in museum-quality woodcrafts is **Artesanías Biesanz** (Biesanz Woodworks) in Escazú. Woodcarver Barry Biesanz supports a country-wide reforestation program and is careful not to work with fresh-cut trees. In his studio/showroom, he and his hand-picked staff create small, high-quality pieces such as jewellery boxes, trays, bowls, and other items whose designs depict Costa Rican folklore.

Sarchí

The nearby mountain village of Sarchí (near Alajuela) is the home of the Costa Rican *carreta,* or oxcart, a national symbol that reflects Costa Rica's heritage, work ethic, and the ingenuity of its people. The carts are now made in replica as decorative pieces, beautifully finished in striking enamel colours.

The Chaverri family—the town's leading oxcart makers—operate a factory and showroom right on the main street. Replica carts of all sizes can be purchased here and will be disassembled and shipped to your home by factory staff.

ENTERTAINMENT

Like shopping, most nightlife of any merit is in San José and the Central Valley metropolitan area.

Nightclubs

First choice for a night out is **Centro Comercial El Pueblo,** catercorner from the landmark Hotel Bougainvillaea on the north side of downtown. Often overlooked by North American travellers, El Pueblo is a slick, one-stop boutique, dining, and nightclub complex that could hold its own in any major city. The place resembles a Spanish village, with tile roofs, attractive patios, and fountains in a garden-like setting. Walkways lead to six discos, five restaurant/bars, and smart, one-of-a-kind shops.

Los Balcones, a small, narrow room, often features a trio from Bolivia playing music from the Andes. Other nights, it might be music from Brazil or Argentina. Nearby, Infinito has the feel of the classic cinematic night clubs where Valentino strutted about and slinky ladies seductively fluttered their eyelashes. Chavetas, also dark and smoochy (one of the few places where Ticos usually wear a coat and tie), is high energy, always busy, and filled with laughter and chatter. Babaloo could be a back room in an old, high-ceilinged hacienda, laid out as it is with a red-brick floor, twirling fans, small black tables, and a tiny bar at the rear. The music draws from bossa nova and Brazil, Costa Rica, and Latin jazz-fusion depending upon the night. The Tango Bar del Che, also dark and cosy, presents traditional music from Argentina. Singing takes the place of dancing.

The Gran Hotel on Plaza de la Cultura is the epicentre for any self-respecting San José boulevardier.

Key Largo, between Avenidas 1 and 3 on Calle 7, across from the Holiday Inn Aurora, is a legendary San José hangout that is bigger than life: a restaurant, a popular nightclub with dancing to a live band, and a second home for women of the night. As one Josefino says bluntly, "Take your choice." Locals like to bring their out-of-town guests here, and travellers drop in throughout the evening to dance and enjoy the food and atmosphere. After 9:00 P.M. there's a small admission fee.

Theatre

The gorgeous **Teatro Melico Salazar,** on Avenida 2 across from Parque Central, is hosting the Orquesta Sinfonía Nacional (National Symphony Orchestra) while the Teatro Nacional is undergoing earthquake repairs. The theatre also offers opera, concerts, musicals, and the colourful Folkloric Fantastic show during the summer months.

The city's lively theatre scene is another way to immerse yourself in the culture and tune in to the Spanish language. Check *Costa Rica Today* and the *Tico Times* newspapers (both English language) for play listings and curtain times.

Casinos

The casinos scattered about San José in the larger hotels are not as high-powered and mechanical as those in Las Vegas, nor as snobby as the ones on the French Riviera. The dealers, after a game of roulette or craps, actually smile when they take your money. Most casinos serve courtesy drinks and are open late.

The **Hotel Herradura,** on the road to the airport 20 minutes from downtown, has a popular European-style casino, as does the adjacent **Cariari Hotel and Country Club.** Both offer live music and dancing. The Cariari's Los Mariscos Bar soothes the high rollers with live music Thursday through Saturday. The casino on the 17th floor of the downtown **Holiday Inn Aurora,** Avenida 5 at Calle 5, is advertised as the highest casino in the world, with the best view.

The **Gran Hotel** has a small but busy casino, as does the **Corobicí Hotel** near La Sabana Park. Adjoining the Corobicí's casino is the hotel's nightclub, which on weekends is extremely crowded. The bar at the left of the entrance is a good place to survey the scene. A doorman, who collects a small cover charge, pretends to screen the patrons but lets everyone in.

EATING OUT

Though it is sometimes said that dining out in Costa Rica—except in one of San José's better-known "International" restaurants—is about as enjoyable as pulling teeth, experienced Costa Rica travellers (and most Ticos) will heartily disagree. It's true that Costa Rica has a slim cookbook and few national dishes, but many local chefs display a grand flair for doing magical things with traditional materials.

Unlike in many Latin-American countries, dinner is the primary meal of the day in Costa Rica. Ticos love to eat, and dining out in the evening plays an important role in their lives. It's a time when the entire family can sit down together, escape the heat of the day, and catch up on events.

Starters

Costa Rican chefs prepare a variety of tasty soups, many similar to those from Mexico (which is ranked among the best soup countries in the world). The fish soups especially

***Local chefs excel when they unite denizens of the deep in a rich* sopas de mariscos.**

(sopas de mariscos), generally a combination of shrimp, corvina (Costa Rica's national fish), lobster, and sometimes scallops, cooked with oodles of black pepper and fresh cilantro, are absolutely mouth watering. Black bean soup is another national speciality. It can be as thick as stew, or a thin consommé with a boiled egg floating in the broth and beans settling to the bottom of the bowl.

Male waiters are called *camarero* (cahmahrayro), female *camarera* (cahmahrayrah).

Hearts-of-palm salad and a similar creation, *cocktail de palmito,* are offered on most menus as appetizers as well. A liberal dousing with spicy salsa/vinegar dressing sets them off nicely. Bananas and plantains are prepared in a variety of ways and are also often presented as hors d'oeuvres.

Main Courses

Of all Costa Rican staples, the most famous is *gallo pinto,* a traditional, unpretentious dish of white rice (*arroz*) and black beans (*frijoles*) prepared with or without spices in a hundred different ways. Calorie-rich and sometimes smothered in sour cream, *gallo pinto* is served throughout the country and around the clock, even for breakfast. It lifts the spirit, fights the blahs, and is a shot of quick energy; if there's a Tico who doesn't eat *gallo pinto* at least once a week, he or she has yet to be heard from.

Add beef, pork, or chicken and a selection of vegetables—ranging from potatoes to bananas—to *gallo pinto,* and you have a *casado* (sort of a Costa Rican combination plate). In most restaurants, one order of *casado* will easily feed two people. Better yet, it's inexpensive. You can normally order *casado* in any restaurant for less than U.S.$3. It is often accompanied by *patacones,* strips of plantain that resemble french-fries that have been baked.

Costa Rica boasts an array of tropical fruits that find their ways into fresh creations called **naturales** *or* **frescos.**

Most restaurants offer a variety of meat (*bistek* or *carne*), chicken (*pollo*), pork (*puerco*), and seafood (*mariscos* or *pescado*) dishes as standard fare. The beef and chicken will often seem overcooked, but only because cattle and chickens here are usually pasture or barnyard raised on natural grasses and seeds, and aren't as tender as the hormone-injected, animal-factory cattle and chickens in the U.S. and elsewhere.

With every meal, you'll normally be served a plate of Costa Rican-style tortillas, tasty (and often sweet) corn pancakes about the size of a man's wallet. If tortillas don't come with your meal, ask for them. Used as a scoop for the *gallo pinto,* or simply eaten with a thick dousing of honey, butter, or salsa, they are scrumptious.

Desserts

The typical dessert in Costa Rica, as in most of Latin America, is flan, a sweet, caramel-flavoured custard usually served cold. You might also want to try the *queque seco,* a dry pound cake often sprinkled with powdered sugar. If you don't have a sweet tooth, order a slab of *palmito,* the famous strained white cheese from Zarcero or Ciudad Quesada. In the highlands they eat it on tortillas with peach preserves slathered on top. Fruit, too, is often served for dessert. Mangos, papayas, pineapple, guavas, and bananas are available fresh, in season.

Meals usually end with a cup of rich Costa Rican coffee, black and heavily sugared. Costa Rican coffee, grown and processed primarily on the lower slopes of the highlands around the Central Valley, is light, rich, and delicious. Unhappily, the best locally produced coffee beans are exported to Europe and the United States. Normally, what you drink in Costa Rican restaurants, or buy in the stores, is second grade. And remember, nothing is rushed, especially not the bill (*la cuenta*).

"Sodas"

Perhaps the most common type of restaurant in Costa Rica is called a *"soda."* Normally quite small with just a few tables, it is a sort of fast-food, family-owned and-operated diner that usually serves basic, inexpensive Costa Rican food. *Sodas* are found virtually everywhere in the country, from the busiest San José street corner to the most remote farming village in the Guanacaste. They are where the locals eat if a more formal setting isn't required. Consequently, some of the best traditional food in Costa Rica is served at these little places, so don't pass them up just because

Cheers! Break the ice over a round of frozen cocktails.

they aren't fancy. For example, there's a tiny *soda* just east of Braulio Carrillo Park that serves the best hamburgers and the most magnificent chicken sandwiches in all of Central America.

Fancier Costa Rican restaurants automatically add a 10 percent tip, called a *propina*, to your bill.

Drinks

Costa Rica has few vineyards, so most of its wines are imported from Argentina or Chile and are relatively expensive (you won't like the locally made wines, so don't bother). There are six or seven locally brewed beers (*cerveza*) in Costa Rica, among them Bavaria, Imperial, Pilsen, Bremen, and Rock Ice. They're all good, at about U.S.$1 per bottle.

Local fruit juice (*naturales* or *frescos*) is healthy and delicious, but make sure it has been squeezed in front of your eyes, or has at least been refrigerated.

Extras

In fancier restaurants, an 11 percent sales tax will be included on your tab, plus a 10 percent tip called a *propina* (watch for the latter in order not to duplicate it). Smaller restaurants in remote areas, however, sometimes do not add a tip to the bill, so if service merits you should add 10 percent.

No-No's

The things not to eat in Costa Rica—as scrumptious as they might look—are fresh salads, uncooked vegetables, and unpeeled fruit. It's also not a good idea to purchase snacks or meals from vendor carts on the street. They may smell great and are undoubtedly tasty, but hot sun and a lack of refrigeration can cause some vendor-sold foods to spoil quickly.

INDEX

HANDY TRAVEL TIPS

An A–Z Summary of Practical Information

A

ACCOMMODATION *(alojamientos)*

Except for the upscale hotels in San José most accommodations in Costa Rica won't be luxurious. On a ranked list of Central American accommodations, however, those of San José and the Central Valley would stand near the top.

Where lodging is concerned in the rest of the country, an apt description might be "moderate"—moderately priced, moderate in physical appearance, and moderate in comfort and standards of service. In most cases, don't expect the sort of establishments you'll find in the United States or Europe; remember, much of Costa Rica is still remote and isolated. In or around the national parks and wildlife reserves, for example, lodges will be comfortable but often without the usual niceties such as room service, ice, and, in some cases, electricity.

The most basic type of accommodations in Costa Rica are *pensións* and *apartotels.* Both are inexpensive and usually offer small single or shared units (generally in urban environments), which may rent for as little as U.S.$4 or $5 a night. Similar types of shelters are *cabinas,* small, basic rooms with sink, bed, and possibly a kitchenette. Seldom do the aforementioned have private bathrooms or air-conditioning.

More expensive and certainly more comfortable is the new generation of bed & breakfast inns (most of them owned by foreigners) popping up all over Costa Rica. If you're interested in staying at a B&B, contact the Costa Rica Bed and Breakfast Group, tel. (506) 223-4168 for more information or reservations.

Room rates have not varied greatly over the past several years, but its wise to double-check before you leave home, and certainly before you pay for anything. Hotels are required to add a huge 18.46 percent in taxes to the room rate. Hotel restaurants (and most other restaurants as well) add 11 percent sales tax and often a 10 percent service charge (*propina*) to the check. Extra gratuities, for exceptional service, are at your discretion. High season is November 1 to April 30; low season is May 1 to October 31.

I'd like a single/ double room...	**Quisiera una habitación sencilla/doble**
...with bath/shower.	**con baño/regadera.**
What's the rate per night?	**¿Cual es el precio por noche?**
Where is there a cheap hotel?	**¿Dónde hay un hotel económico?**

AIRPORTS *(aeropuerto)*

All international flights arrive and leave from Juan Santamaría International Airport about 20 kms (12 miles) northwest of San José in the city of Alajuela. Sansa Airways, one of two small Costa Rican domestic airlines, operates from the Domestic Terminal at Juan Santamaría International. The other domestic carrier, Travelair, arrives and departs from Tobías Bolaños Airport in Pavas, a suburb of San José.

Taxi drivers hawk their services right outside the terminal building, and there's never a lack of available cabs. Taxis are efficient and clean, but most cabbies drive like the wind and don't use their meters, so establish the fare in advance. Drivers readily accept U.S. dollars, but if you become confused with the Spanish numbers write the fare down on paper for verification (a solid safeguard that removes the stress of dealing with street-wise cabbies). A cab ride into the downtown area shouldn't cost more than U.S.$15; the trip takes about 20 minutes.

The Tuasa bus company offers non-stop service between the airport and downtown San José. Buses depart every 15 minutes during peak-arrival periods from outside the terminal just behind the car-rental counters. The trip to the Plaza de la Cultura takes about 30 minutes if traffic isn't too heavy; bus fares are modest.

Porter!	**¡Maletero!**
Where's the bus for ...?	**¿Dónde está el camión para...?**

B

BICYCLE RENTAL *(renta de bicicletas)*

Ecotreks is probably the best-known biking/adventure tour operator in Costa Rica; tel. (506) 228-4029; fax (506) 289-8191.

BUDGETING FOR YOUR TRIP

Food is a real bargain throughout the country, with handicrafts a close second. You can find adequate lodging for U.S.$20 a night, and eat well for less than U.S.$5 a meal.

CAMPING *(campismo)*

A handful of organized campgrounds, most of them rustic and off the beaten path, are scattered throughout Costa Rica, especially near coasts and national parks (some national parks do not allow camping within their boundaries, so be sure to check first). Wet weather, snakes, insects, and lack of facilities, however, can make camping out here a less than paradisiacal experience. Sleeping on some beaches is allowed, but be wary of freak waves and nocturnal reptiles that search for food at night on the sand.

May we camp here?	**¿Podemos acampar aquí?**
We have a tent/trailer.	**Tenemos una tienda de caravana/campaña**

CLIMATE

Perhaps the best way to deal with the climate when traveling throughout Costa Rica is to expect warm weather and be prepared for rain.

For the most part, the temperature range across Costa Rica varies from mild (15–20°C, 59–68°F) to hot (30s°C, high 80s–low 100s°F). In the mountains and cloud forests, evenings and nighttime hours can be cool. The dampness may add to the sense of chill, but even in these areas the temperature can hardly be described as cold. On rare occasions the temperature may drop to around freezing, but generally a fire in the hearth of a mountain lodge is more for ambiance than relief from the cold.

The two principal seasons are distinguished by differences in humidity and precipitation rather than temperature. The rainy season, *invierno,* runs from May through November. The dry season, *verano,* runs from December through April.

Any generalities in Costa Rica, however, must be qualified with the specifics of microclimates that prevail across the country. Rainy conditions are more prevalent on the Caribbean side of the Continental Divide and can push the envelope on either side of the May–November rainy season. On the Pacific coast the north is drier, the south wetter.

Average Daily Temperatures in San José

	J	F	M	A	M	J	J	A	S	O	N	D
Min °C	14	14	15	17	17	17	17	16	16	16	16	14
°F	58	58	59	62	62	62	62	61	61	60	60	58
Max °C	24	24	26	26	27	26	25	26	26	25	25	24
°F	75	75	79	79	80	80	77	78	79	77	77	75

CLOTHING

The climate in most of Costa Rica for most of the year is moderately warm to hot, so light cotton clothing is usually perfect for most situations.

During the rainy season and in the more humid sections of the country—the southern Pacific coast and the Caribbean lowlands — prepare to get wet. How you prepare is pretty much your call. While such conditions would normally suggest foul-weather gear (slickers, ponchos, or raincoats), the rain is often accompanied by some of the hottest temperatures, and rain gear tends to hold in the heat. Another option is simply to get wet. On jaunts through the steamier rain forests, for example, old clothing and all-weather sandals that dry quickly are a viable alternative to rain gear. Umbrellas are useless. If you prepare mentally for the eventuality—if not the certainty—of being soaked, then you'll do just fine.

In the cooler environments of the cloud forests and central highlands, rain gear makes perfect sense. The ceaseless soaking and lower temperatures there may make you grateful for some rain protection and heat containment. A sweater or light-to mid-weight jacket may come in handy, too, particularly in the evenings and early mornings.

Protection from the sun is important on Costa Rica's beaches, where it can shine for long periods. Sunscreen, wide-brimmed hats, beach wraps, and other protective garb should be a part of every beach-goer's arsenal. Many beaches are rimmed by lovely stands of trees, and you should take full advantage of the shade they afford.

As for dress requirements, Costa Rica is a very informal place. Ties, jackets, and cocktail gowns are seldom worn here, even by the Ticos. If you're in doubt about a restaurant, theatre, or dinner party, however, simply call and inquire.

CRIME

Flaunting expensive jewellery, cameras, luggage, or rolls of cash may produce the same problems in Costa Rica as on a street corner in Manhattan, Los Angeles, London, or Frankfurt. Costa Rica is not considered a high-crime country, but a lack of common sense will bring out the criminals here, too. Be especially alert for pickpockets and purse-snatchers in the more crowded metropolitan areas, especially San José, Puntarenas, and Puerto Limón.

Car theft is a problem in some areas, particularly the theft of rental vehicles. Use sound judgment before you leave a vehicle on a secluded rural road (especially in the national parks); when you're in an unfamiliar town or village, ask at hotels and restaurants about sensible precautions.

If you are the victim of a theft, a mugging, or a burglary, contact the nearest police station (tel. 911 in San José; 117 for the rest of the country). This will be important for insurance claims, even if it doesn't result in the recovery of your lost property.

CUSTOMS *(aduana)* and ENTRY FORMALITIES

Entry into Costa Rica is permitted with a passport and a tourist card; the latter costs about U.S.$5 and can be obtained at any Costa Rican consulate and from most airlines that serve the country. You must also present a round-trip airline ticket as evidence that you do not intend to make your stay a permanent one.

Citizens of the United States, Canada, the United Kingdom, and the Irish Republic may enter the country without a visa for a period of 90 days or less. Citizens of Australia, New Zealand and South Africa may enter the country without a visa for up to 30 days

Duty-free allowance. Visitors may bring 500 cigarettes or 500 grams of tobacco, and three liters of wine or spirits, into Costa Rica; also two cameras, plus personal electronic equipment (laptop computer, tape recorder, etc.) and items not for sale. Visitors may take anything they wish out of Costa Rica, including currency, so long as it isn't illegal in the U.S. or other home country.

I have nothing to declare. **No tengo nada que declarar.**

DRIVING IN COSTA RICA

Driving in Costa Rica is not recommended for visitors. However, many visitors do drive, and if you are one of them, the best word of advice is to use extreme caution and to drive defensively — Costa Rica has one of the world's highest auto accident rates. A Costa Rica driver's license isn't required unless you plan to spend more than three months in the country or state. Driving is on the right-hand side of the road. Regulations concerning traffic lights, road signs, passing, yielding to pedestrians, etc., are similar to those in the United States, Canada, and Europe.

The speed limit on major highways is 80km/hr (50mph). For primary and secondary roads it varies between 40km/hr (25mph) and 60km/hr (37mph).

In the cities, if you're a pedestrian, don't assume that a red light necessarily means oncoming traffic is going to stop for you. Make sure the coast is clear before stepping off the curb.

E

ELECTRIC CURRENT

Electric current is 110-volt, 60-cycle AC (the same as in North America). Travellers whose portable appliances do not run on that current should bring their own adapters. Most accommodations do not have the equipment needed to convert power. Sockets and plugs are of the type used in the United States and Canada.

EMBASSIES and CONSULATES *(embajadas y consuladas)*

Canada: Oficentro Ejecutivo La Sabana, Edificio 5, 3rd Floor, Detras La Contraloria, Sabana Sur. Tel. (506) 296-4149; fax (506) 296-4270.

Great Britain: Paseo Colón, Calle 38 and 40, Edificio Centro Colón. Tel. (506) 221-5566; fax (506) 233-9938.

United States: Carretera Pavas en frente del Centro Commercial. Tel. (506) 220-3939; fax (506) 220-2305.

EMERGENCIES *(emergencias)*

The general emergency telephone number is 911 in San José and the surrounding Central Valley. To reach the nearest police department (*policía*) in other parts of Costa Rica, dial 117; to reach the nearest fire department (*bomberos*), dial 118.

G

GAY & LESBIAN TRAVELLERS

There is a gay community in San José, but police often harass the patrons of gay and lesbian bars and clubs, which are sometimes raided. For information on gay activities in Costa Rica, or for a list of hotels and restaurants that cater to gays, contact the organization Triangulo Rosa, Apdo. 1619-4050, in Alajuela, Costa Rica; tel. (506) 234-1370, fax (506) 234-2411.

GETTING THERE

There is direct air service to Juan Santamaría International Airport from eight U.S. gateways: New York, Miami, New Orleans, Houston, Los Angeles, Orlando, San Francisco, and San Juan, Puerto Rico. Of the U.S. carriers, Continental and American have the most experienced personnel and offer the most extensive connecting patterns for their direct and nonstop services from major U.S. airports.

The following airlines fly to and from Costa Rica: LACSA, the international airline of Costa Rica, operates between Juan Santamaría and Miami, New Orleans, New York, Los Angeles, San Francisco, and San Juan; tel. 800-225-2272. American Airlines has direct service to and from Miami International, and connecting service to its vast system throughout the U.S.; tel. 800-433-7300. Continental Airlines offers direct service to and from Houston; tel. 800-231-0856. Delta Airlines has direct service to and from Orlando; tel. 800-221-1212. Mexicana has direct service to and from Los Angeles International, and also has connecting service from several U.S. cities, via Mexico City; in the U.S., tel. 800-531-7921; in Canada, tel. 800-531-7923. SAHSA, the national airline of Honduras, has service to and from Miami, New Orleans, and Houston; tel. 800-327-1225. TACA, based in El Salvador, has direct service to and from Houston; it offers connecting service to and from New York's JFK, Washington Dulles Airport, Miami, and New Orleans; tel.

800-535-8780. United offers direct service to and from Miami; tel. 800-241-6522.

Visitors traveling from Canada, Australia, and Europe usually connect to one of the above carriers, often in Miami. Travel agents and tour operators create packages that include air transportation, accommodations, tours, and assorted extras; consult your travel agent or the reservations desks of the above carriers for details. There are also KLM, Iberia, and charter flights available from The Netherlands, Spain, and Germany to Costa Rica; ask your travel agent.

Several international ocean-going cruise lines call at both Puerto Limón on the Caribbean coast and Puerto Caldera on the Pacific coast, but seldom stay for more than a day. They provide packaged tours to sightseeing and shopping areas. Dockside, you can cut your own deal for a day trip into the national parks or preserves with a cab or local guide, but that will take some negotiating. Ask your travel agent for a list of cruise lines currently stopping in Costa Rica.

The Inter-American Highway (formerly called the Pan-American Highway and in Costa Rica officially known as the Autopista Florencio del Castillo Norte) enters Costa Rica from Nicaragua in the north at Peñas Blancas and exits in the south at Paso Canoas on the Panamanian border. There are other border-crossing points for Nicaragua and Panamá, but they are reached effectively only in four-wheel-drive vehicles. You must clear customs and immigration at both points.

GUIDES *(guías)* and TOURS

If you're in the market for a day trip only, probably the best place to arrange for a local guide is the concierge desk at your hotel. Try to give the concierge at least a 24-hour advance notice; most day trips, especially those to the volcanoes and other attractions around San José, leave early in the morning.

Many taxi drivers also double as guides, but taxi-tours are usually far more expensive than a full- or half-day trip booked through a local guide service. If you do use a cab, make sure the driver speaks understandable English, and negotiate the full fare before you leave the hotel (get it in writing).

For multi-day trips, there are a number of Costa Rica based guide services and tour companies that offer organized excursions to all of the country's major attractions. Below is a list of the largest and most respected:

Adventuras Naturales: Tel. (506) 225-3939; fax (506) 253-6934

Aggressor Fleet: Tel. 504-385-2628 (in the U.S.)

Costa Rica Expeditions: Tel. (506) 257-0766; fax (506) 257-1665

Costa Rica Sun Tours: Tel. (506) 255-3418; fax (506) 255-4410

Costa Rica Whitewater: Tel. (506) 257-0766; fax (506) 257-1665

Ecotreks: Tel. (506) 228-4029; fax (506) 289-8191

Geotur: Tel. (506) 227-4029; fax (506) 253-6338

Horizones: Tel. (506) 222-2022; fax (506) 255-4513

Jungle Trails: Tel. (506) 255-3486; fax (506) 255-2782

Ríos Tropicales: Tel. (506) 233-6455; fax (506) 255-4354

Serendipity Adventures: Tel. (506) 450-0328; no fax

Swiss Travel: Tel. (506) 231-4055; fax (506) 231-3030

Temptress Cruises: Tel. (506) 232-6672; fax: (506) 220-2103; in the U.S., tel. 800-336-8423 or 305-871-2663; fax 305-871-2657

Tropical Bungee: Tel. (506) 235-6455; no fax

If your plans include an extended stay on the Pacific coasts, you might want to contact Temptress Cruises, a local cruise-ship operator that offers packages—from 4 days to 1½ weeks—exploring the Pacific coast's national parks and nature reserves. They depart from the Pacific port city of Puntarenas (but will arrange transportation from San José). Given the difficulty of covering this expansive coastline by land, a cruise is a great way to see the flora and fauna of this biologically diverse country.

We'd like an English-speaking guide.	**Queremos un guía que hable inglés.**
I need an English interpreter.	**Necesito un intérprete de inglés.**

H

HEALTH and MEDICAL CARE

Costa Rica is considered one of the most medically advanced nations in Latin America. If you have a medical emergency you'll probably be in better hands here than anywhere else in Central America. If you want to take extra precautions, and if your insurance does not cover you when traveling abroad, consider buying medical insurance before you leave your home country; some policies provide for evacuation by air if you get sick or have an accident.

In the major metropolitan areas of Costa Rica—San José, Alajuela, Heredia, and Cartago—the drinking water is generally considered safe. In the countryside or in lightly populated beach areas, however, it can be suspect.

Insects constitute the greatest health problem in the country, particularly in the lowland rain forests and marshes. Swarms of mosquitoes are not uncommon during the rainy season, and they will feast on your blood if you don't wear repellent or long-sleeved garments. Disease from such bites is rare, although people contract malaria in various lowland areas from time to time, particularly on the Caribbean side of the country. If you're concerned, consult your physician before leaving home.

Drowning is probably the greatest actual threat to visitors. Some of the most popular beach areas in the country can be hazardous if you ignore your limitations as a swimmer. Riptides are a factor in most of the 200 drowning deaths that occur each year. If you're caught in such a current, don't fight it; many riptide drownings result from exhaustion. Instead, ride the current out until it dissipates, then swim back at a 45-degree angle to the shore, to minimize being caught in the current again. It is a good rule of thumb always to swim with a buddy and never to swim while intoxicated. On the Caribbean side of the country sharks can be a problem, sometimes following the lower orders of the food chain close to shore and even into the deeper channels of the estuaries and swamps.

Protection from the sun is important on Costa Rica's beaches. Wide-brimmed hats and beach wraps are recommended, as is a high-numbered sunscreen.

During hikes through the woods you should be aware of possible encounters with dangerous animals, especially venomous spiders and snakes. The *barba amarilla* is a particularly nasty snake that has accounted for the greatest percentage of the human deaths from snakebite. It can grow to a length of up to 2½ metres (8 feet) and is generally hard to spot because of its neutral—gray, olive-green, and brown—colors. Snakes seek out the warmth of beaches and the packed earth of hiking trails during the night; you should watch out for them in these areas, particularly during early-morning treks.

water	**agua**
purified water	**agua purificada**
a bottle of mineral water	**una botella de agua mineral**
carbonated/non-carbonated	**con gas/sin gas**

HOLIDAYS *(días festivos)*

Costa Ricans like to celebrate. The country's national holidays are:

1 January	*Año Nuevo*	New Year's Day
19 March	*Día de San José*	San José Day
March or April	*Jueves Santo*	Holy Thursday (movable date)
March or April	*Viernes Santo*	Good Friday (movable date)
March or April	*Pascua*	Easter (movable date)

11 April	*Día de Juan Santamaría*	Juan Santamaría Day
1 May	*Día del Trabajo*	Labor Day
29 June	*Día de San Pedro y San Pablo*	Saints Peter and Paul Day
25 July	*Día de la Anexión de Guanacaste*	Guanacaste Annexation Day
2 August	*Día de la Virgen de Los Angeles*	Virgin of Los Angeles Day (feast of the country's patron saint)
15 August	*Día de las Madres*	Mother's Day
15 September	*Día de la Independencia*	Independence Day
12 October	*Día de la Raza*	Columbus Day
8 December	*La Fiesta de la Inmaculada Concepción*	Feast of the Immaculate Conception
25 December	*Navidad*	Christmas Day

LANGUAGE

Spanish is Costa Rica's principal (and official) language, but in the Central Valley's metro area, many Ticos—especially those involved in tourism—speak English. On the Caribbean coast, the large Rastafarian population speaks both English and Creole, the latter a rapid and virtually indecipherable (to outsiders, at least) mixture of Spanish and English. Several Indian languages—the most common being Bribrí—are spoken in remote areas of the Talamanca Mountains.

Spanish-language programs are popular with some visitors to Costa Rica, and often regular sightseeing tours can be combined with intensive language workshops. For more information on these programs, contact one of the following: Centro Linguistico Conversa, Apdo. 17-1007, San José, tel. (506) 221-

7649, or in the U.S. (800) 354-5036, fax (506) 233-2418; Centro Cultural Costarricense Norteamericano, Apdo. 1489-1000, San José, tel. (506) 225-9433, fax (506) 224-1480; Central American Institute for International Affairs, Apdo. 10302-1000, San José, tel. (506) 233-8571, fax (506) 221-5238.

Good morning/day	**Buenos días**
Good afternoon/evening	**Buenas tardes**
Good night	**Buenas noches**
Good-bye	**Adíos**
See you later	**Hasta luego**
Please	**Por favor**
Thank you	**Gracias**

LAUNDRY and DRY-CLEANING

For several reasons, most experienced Costa Rica travellers carry enough clothing to see them through their entire trip. First, laundry and dry-cleaning establishments are hard to find, even in San José and especially so in outlying areas. Second, although many hotels will do your laundry on request, you may not get your clothing back for several days.

M

MAPS

The best general road map of Costa Rica available is a 1:500,000 publication, available from International Travel Map Productions, P.O. Box 2290, Vancouver, B.C., V6B 3W5, Canada. It is difficult to find in Costa Rica itself. Another source (for all publishers) is Treaty Oak, P.O. Box 50295, Austin, Texas 78763; tel. (512) 326-4141, fax (512) 443-0973.

MEDIA

The *Tico Times,* published once a week and available at most newsstands in metro San José, Cartago, Alajuela, and Heredia, is the most widely read English-language newspaper in the country. Another such weekly is *Costa Rica Today,* which caters mostly to vacationing tourists in search of events.

For news most visitors prefer to watch CNN International, available in the better hotels.

MONEY MATTERS

Costa Rican currency (*moneda*). The official monetary unit for Costa Rica is the *colón.* But because the rate of exchange rate fluctuates wildly sometimes against foreign currencies and because many Costa Rican hotels and resorts have bases in the United States, all prices in this book are quoted in U.S. dollars. Dollars are widely accepted (and other foreign currencies can be exchanged), though using *colones* will save you from having to calculate and round off each transaction and, over the course of your visit, probably will save you money. Bills come in denominations of 10, 20, 50, 100, 500, 1000, and 5000. Coins come in denominations of 1, 2, 5, 10, 20, 50, and 100 *colones.* One *colón* is 100 *centimos; centimos* come in 25 and 50 coins.

Currency exchange and traveller's checks (*cheque de viaje*). You can exchange money at the airport, at banks (*bancos*), and in most major hotels. Traveller's checks from major companies are widely accepted. ATM machines exist in some of the larger banks, but are rare, and many limit withdrawals.

There has been a recent rash of counterfeit U.S.$100 bills being passed in Costa Rica, and many businesses now refuse to accept them. To save yourself potential trouble, if you're carrying cash carry nothing larger than U.S.$50 bills instead. And get rid of old, torn, or crumpled bills, no matter what type of currency they are. Most Costa Rican banks and businesses will not accept anything less than crisp, reasonably new banknotes.

Credit cards (*tarjeta de crédito*). The big three international credit cards—American Express, Visa, and MasterCard—are accepted by an ever-increasing number of businesses throughout Costa Rica, including the major transportation, accommodations, food and beverage, and shopping establishments. Check before booking or ordering if unsure.

I want to change some dollars/pounds	**Quiero cambiar dólares/libras/esterlinas.**
Do you accept traveller's checks?	**¿Acepta usted cheques de viajero?**
Can I pay with this credit card?	**¿Puedo pagar con esta tarjeta de crédito?**
How much does it cost?	**¿Cuánto es?**
Do you have anything cheaper?	**¿Tiene algo más barato?**

OPENING HOURS

Most government offices are open from 8:00 A.M. to 4:00 P.M., Monday through Friday. Banks are open 9:00 A.M. to 3:00 P.M., Monday through Friday, but some branches stay open until 6:00 or 6:30 P.M.; some are also open for a half day on Saturday.

The shopping day in general runs from 8:00 A.M. to 7:00 P.M., with a lunch break or siesta from noon to 2:00 P.M.

POLICE *(policía)*

If you're robbed, mugged, or become a victim of any other type of crime in Costa Rica, you can file a report with the Organismo de Investigacíon Judicial in the Supreme Court Building, Avenida 6, Calle 17 and 19 in San José, tel. (506) 255-0122.

The general emergency number in San José and the Central Valley is 911. In the rest of Costa Rica it is 117.

POST OFFICES *(correo)*

For usual post office business, it's probably best to use the main post office (*Correo Central*) in whatever city you happen to be. In San José, the main post office is located downtown on Calle 2, Avenida 1 and 3. They also offer telegraph service.

For postcards and letters home, better hotels or hotel gift shops usually sell airmail stamps and offer mail-drop boxes. Airmail letters to the U.S. cost about 30 cents, and to Europe about 40 cents.

I want to send a telegram to ...	**Quisiera mandar un telegrama a ...**
Have you received any mail for ... ?	**¿Ha recibido correo para ... ?**
stamp/letter/postcard	**timbre/carta/tarjeta**
special delivery (express)	**urgente**
airmail	**correo aéreo**
registered	**registrado**

PUBLIC TRANSPORTATION

Bus service of one kind or another is available in most towns and cities in Costa Rica, and almost everywhere else. Buses (*guaguas, autobús*) are the major method of transportation for hundreds of thousands of Ticos, and if you're on a tight budget it is the way to travel. You might be cramped (or have to share a seat with a goat or a few chickens occasionally), and space for luggage is limited, but for the most part Costa Rican buses are clean and efficient. Fares are extremely modest; for less than U.S.$10 you can go almost anywhere in the country.

One drawback to riding buses, unfortunately, is that central bus terminals do not exist, not even in San José. Most routes originate and end at the main office of the particular bus company or at bus stops (many of them unmarked) along the streets and highways, so you need to know where you're going and which company provides service to that area (you can buy a ticket from the driver as you board). General information is available from the Costa Rican Tourist Board; for more details about which buses run where, ask at your hotel or contact the individual bus companies.

T

TELEPHONE *(teléfono)*

Costa Rica was one of the last countries in Latin America to modernize its telephone system, but it now has one of the best in the region; all local telephone numbers now have seven digits. The country code for Costa Rica is 506. City codes and area codes are not used. From the United States and Europe, you can direct dial any number in Costa Rica by dialing the international access code + 506 + the seven-digit local number.

Pay phones are common throughout the country and are generally in good working order. The cost for a local call is 10 *colones,* but most booths will accept 5, 10, and 20 *colón* coins. To dial any number in Costa Rica, simply deposit 10 *colones,* then dial the seven-digit number. Local information is 113.

To make a collect call or a credit-card call to the United States or Europe, you'll be better off connecting to an international carrier and charging the call to your long-distance calling card (it's difficult to pay for an international call by feeding 10-*colones* coins into a slot). You can make operator-assisted international calls from most hotels, but the charges may quadruple.

TIME DIFFERENCES

Costa Rica is on North America's Central Standard Time (for example, Chicago), which is Greenwich Mean Time minus six hours. Because Costa Rica is close to the Equator, the number of daylight hours does not vary from season to season as greatly as in the more northern or southern regions of the hemisphere. For most of the year there are 12 hours of daylight, from about 6:00 A.M. to 6:00 P.M. Costa Rica does not observe Daylight Saving Time. Here are the time differences during standard time periods:

San José	New York	London	Jo'burg	Sydney	Auckland
6:00 A.M.	7:00 A.M.	noon	2:00 P.M.	9:00 P.M.	11:00 P.M.

TIPPING

Most large restaurants add a 10 percent service charge to the bill, so further tipping isn't necessary unless the service was really excellent. If it was, another 5 percent is more than adequate. In smaller, less-expensive restaurants, a service charge might not be automatically added.

Bellboys normally get 50 to 75 U.S. cents a bag, depending upon the quality of the hotel. Taxi drivers don't usually expect tips, but if they've been especially helpful an extra 75 U.S. cents will certainly be appreciated.

Tips for tour guides vary from region to region, but standard practice is U.S.$4–$5 per day per person. Bus drivers usually get U.S.$2–$3 per day per person.

TOILETS *(baños, sanitarios)*

Public toilets are rare in Costa Rica, but in a pinch you can always ask to use the facilities in a restaurant or store. Be aware, however, that they won't always be clean, and some won't have toilet paper (it's always a good idea to carry a small packet of toilet paper or tissues with you while sightseeing or shopping).

Where are the toilets? **¿Dónde están los sanitarios?**

TOURIST INFORMATION OFFICES *(oficina de turismo)*

The Costa Rican Tourist Board—or, as it's known locally, the Instituto Costarricense de Turismo (ICT)—has offices in Costa

Rica and the United States. The **U.S.** office is located at 1101 Brickel Ave, BIV Tower, Ste. 801, Miami, FL 33131; tel. (800) 327-7033 or (305) 358-2150.

While there are no Costa Rican Tourist Board offices in Europe or Canada, visitors can contact the embassy or consulate (if there is one) in their country of origin.

Canada: 135 York Street, #208, Ottawa K1N 5T, Canada; tel. (613) 562-2855.

U.K.: Flat 1, 14 Lancaster Gate, London W23LH, England; tel. (0171) 705-8844.

Information and materials (in English) are available on a walk-in basis at the ICT office on the Plaza de la Cultura, on Calle 5 between Avenida Central and Avenida 2, in San José; tel. (506) 222-1090. There is also an ICT information counter at Juan Santamaría International Airport. The offices are open during standard government office business hours, 8:00 A.M. to 4:00 P.M., Monday to Friday.

Or, you can write or fax for brochures and other advance information to the ICT at Apartado 777-1000, San José; fax (506) 223-5452.

TRAVELLERS WITH DISABILITIES

Costa Rica is not particularly well-equipped for travellers with disabilities, though this is beginning to change. Some hotels may provide wheelchair access, which often means they have a ramp leading to the lobby and first floor. Be sure to inquire specifically about what facilities really are available when booking a hotel room, restaurant table, or tour.

WEIGHTS and MEASURES

Costa Rica uses the metric system, i.e. metres, kilos, kilometres, etc.

Length

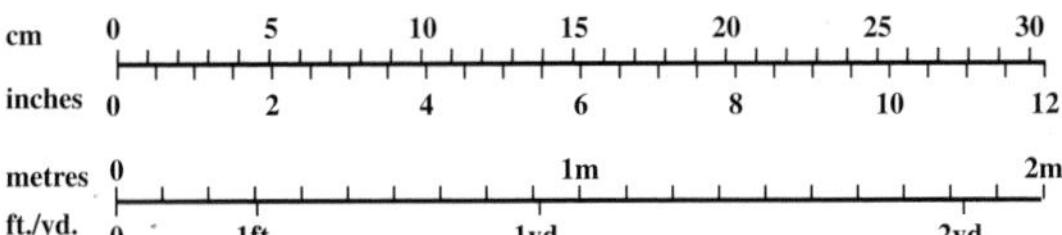

Weight

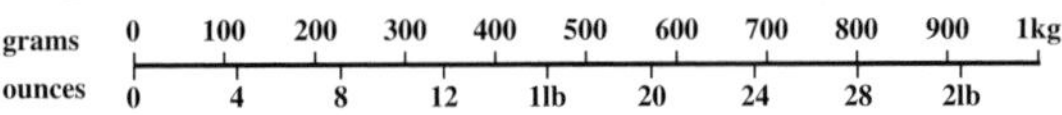

Fluid measures

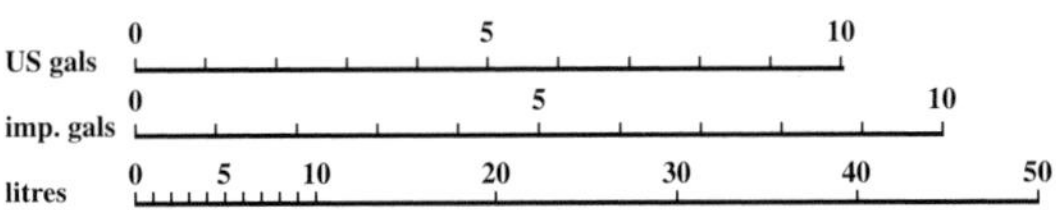

Distance

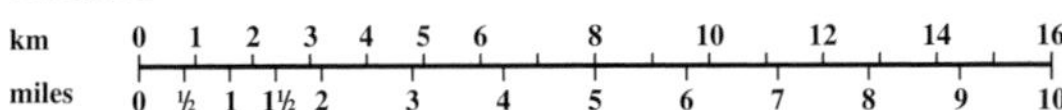

YOUTH HOSTELS *(albergue para jóvenes)*

For a list of youth hostels and prices in Costa Rica, contact The Hostel Toruma, Avenida Central, Calle 29 and 31, San José; tel. (506) 234-8186, fax (506) 224-4085. Hostel Toruma is the clearing house for all hostels in Costa Rica.

SOME USEFUL EXPRESSIONS

Months of the Year

January	**enero**	July	**julio**
February	**febrero**	August	**agosto**
March	**marzo**	September	**septiembre**
April	**abril**	October	**octubre**
May	**mayo**	November	**noviembre**
June	**junio**	December	**diciembre**

Days of the Week

Sunday	**domingo**
Monday	**lunes**
Tuesday	**martes**
Wednesday	**miércoles**
Thursday	**jueves**
Friday	**viernes**
Saturday	**sábado**

Numbers

0	**cero**	16	**dieciséis**
1	**uno**	17	**diecisiete**
2	**dos**	18	**dieciocho**
3	**tres**	19	**diecinueve**
4	**cuatro**	20	**veinte**
5	**cinco**	30	**treinta**
6	**seis**	40	**cuarenta**
7	**siete**	50	**cincuenta**
8	**ocho**	60	**sesenta**
9	**nueve**	70	**setenta**
10	**diez**	80	**ochenta**
11	**once**	90	**noventa**
12	**doce**	100	**cien**
13	**trece**	101	**ciento uno**
14	**catorce**	500	**quinientos**
15	**quince**	1,000 (*1.000*)	**mil**

Recommended Hotels

Recommended hotels are listed by region, in alphabetical order. The more remote locations often do not have street addresses. Locals can tell you where they are, and we've given reservation addresses, usually in a nearby city. You'll find every kind of accommodation in Costa Rica, from cosy, beachside thatch-roofed cabañas to jungle lodges built on stilts to (much less commonly) plush high-rise hotels offering every amenity. We have provided a representative range of these lodgings.

Note that high season in Costa Rica is from November 1 to April 30, and low season is from May 1 to October 31. During the low season, rooms prices may be discounted by as much as 40 percent. The symbols below indicate the price of a double room in high season.

❁❁❁❁	more than U.S.$100
❁❁❁	U.S.$70–100
❁❁	U.S.$40–70
❁	less than U.S.$40

San José (Downtown)

Barceló Amón Plaza ❁❁❁❁ *Avenida 11, Calle 3 bis; tel. (506) 257-0191, fax (506) 257-0284. Mail: Apdo. 4192-1000, San José.* Located in San José's historic Amón district, the Barceló Amón Plaza is expensive but worth every penny. Air-conditioned oversized deluxe rooms and suites. All the usual amenities plus 2-line direct-dial phones, voice mail, data port, and laundry service. Wheelchair access. 90 rooms. Major credit cards.

Gran Hotel Costa Rica ❁❁❁ *Avenida 2 between Calles 1 and 3; tel. (506) 221-4000, fax (506) 221-3501.* Overlooking the Plaza de la Cultura and the Teatro Nacional, the Gran Hotel is smack in the middle of the action. Carpeted, air-conditioned rooms, 24-hour room service, and a popular lobby casino. The outdoor café in front is the best people-watching spot in town. Wheelchair access. 113 rooms. Major credit cards.

Grano de Oro ✿✿✿ *No. 251 Calle 30 between Avenidas 2 & 4; tel. (506) 255-3322, fax (506) 221-2782.* A former private residence recently converted into one of the country's best boutique hotels. Offers a pleasant atmosphere with interior courtyards, warm pastel colours, hanging plants, twirling ceiling fans, and wicker chairs. A sun deck with two hot-tubs has views of Poás, Barva, and Irazú volcanoes. 35 rooms. Major credit cards.

Hotel Bienvenido ✿ *Calle 10, Avenida 1 and 3; tel. (506) 233-2161, fax (506) 221-1872. Mail: Apdo. 389-2200, San José.* Once a movie theatre, this hotel is basic but clean and comfortable. One of the best accommodations in town for those on a tight budget. Some shared baths, depending upon room price. 48 rooms. Major credit cards.

Britannia Hotel ✿✿✿ *Calle 3 and Avenida 11; tel. (506) 223-6667, fax (506) 223-6411. Mail: Apdo. 3742-1000, San José.* This restored colonial mansion has grown into one of the nicest small luxury hotels in downtown San José. Some rooms come with fans, the rest have air conditioning. Attractive atrium restaurant. Helpful staff and courteous service make this a great base in the city. Wheelchair access. 24 rooms. Major credit cards.

Hotel Don Carlos ✿✿ *No. 799 Calle 9, between Avenidas 7 and 9; tel. (506) 221-6707, fax (506) 255-0828. Mail in the U.S.: Dept. 1686, P.O. Box 025216, Miami, FL 33102-5216.* Another remodeled mansion, tastefully done. The indoor patio and garden is a quiet relief from the noise outside. Live music some nights. The hotel has a top-notch gift shop. Continental breakfast included. 36 rooms. Major credit cards.

Hotel Santo Tomas ✿✿ *Avenida 7, Calle 3 and 5; tel. (506) 255-0448, fax (506) 222-3950.* A very comfortable small hotel, close to everything. American owned, in a renovated, early-20th-century home set back from the street. Lots of antiques; a bar but no restaurant (though a Continental breakfast is included). 20 rooms. No credit cards.

San José (Vicinity)

Barceló San José Palacio ❁❁❁❁ *On the General Cañas Highway in La Uruca; tel. (506) 220-2034, fax (506) 220-2036. Mail: Apdo. 458-1150, Robledal de la Uruca, San José.* An 8-floor hotel with luxurious, air-conditioned rooms, formal restaurant, pool-side grill, and tennis, racquetball, and squash courts. Complimentary Continental breakfast with some rooms. 20 minutes from the airport. 255 rooms. Major credit cards.

Camino Real Inter-Continental ❁❁❁❁ *In front of the Multiplaza Shopping Center in Escazú; tel. (506) 289-7000, fax (506) 289-8930. Mail: Apdo. 1856-1000, San José.* Offers 261 deluxe rooms, gourmet restaurant, sauna, casino, and all the other luxuries of a fine hotel. Adjacent to Costa Rica's largest mall. Wheelchair access. Major credit cards.

Meliá Cariari Hotel & Golf Resort ❁❁❁❁ *General Cañas Highway, at Ciudad Cariari; tel. (506) 239-0022, fax (506) 239-2803. Mail: Apdo. 737-1007 Centro Colón, San José.* The place for active, sports-minded travelers who like golf, tennis, and swimming. Presidents Carter, Reagan, and Bush have stayed here. King-sized beds, all the amenities. Wheelchair access. 244 rooms. Major credit cards.

Marriott Hotel and Resort ❁❁❁❁ *Just off the General Cañas Highway in San Antonio de Belén; tel. (506) 298-0000, fax (506) 298-0011. Mail: Apdo. 502-4005, San Antonio de Belén.* A 16th-century hacienda-style hotel set in a coffee plantation. Two outdoor pools, a giant Jacuzzi, tennis courts, driving range, jogging paths, and health club. Several excellent dining options and a popular piano bar. 252 rooms. Wheelchair access. Major credit cards.

Hampton Airport Inn ❁❁ *General Cañas Highway near the airport; tel. (506) 443-0043, fax (506) 442-9532. Mail: Apdo. 195-4003, San José.* Dependable budget chain hotel with swimming pool and airport shuttle. A good place for travelers who are leaving on early flights. Continental breakfast included. Wheelchair access.100 rooms. Major credit cards.

Hotel Herradura ❁❁❁❁ *General Cañas Highway in Ciudad Cariari; tel. (506) 239-0033, fax (506) 239-2292. Mail: Apdo. 7-1880-1000, San José.* A popular resort hotel offering all the usual amenities. Three restaurants, a lively, lobby bar, European-style casino, tennis courts, and privileges at the neighboring Cariari golf course. Wheelchair access. 234 rooms. Major credit cards.

Caribbean Coast South (Puerto Limón, Cahuita, Puerto Viejo)

Aviarios del Caribe ❁❁ *Twenty-one miles south of Puerto Limón; tel. and fax (506) 382-1335. Mail: Apdo. 569-7300, Puerto Limón.* This comfortable bed and breakfast is nestled on the banks of a lush estuary. No air-conditioning, but each spacious room comes equipped with a fan. The surrounding rain forest and waterways are home to more than 300 bird species and other wildlife, viewable on boat tours and along a network of maintained trails. 6 rooms. Major credit cards.

Atlantida Lodge ❁❁ *Cahuita; tel. (506) 755-0115, fax (506) 755-0213. Mail: Atlantida Lodge, Cahuita, Costa Rica.* Lots of lawns and garden greenery here, and the beach is just across the street. *Cabinas* are thatch-roofed, with bamboo dividers and tile floors. No air-conditioning, but all rooms have fans. There's a pool and plenty of tour and activity options. An open-air restaurant serves both local and Continental food. 30 rooms. Major credit cards.

Magellan Inn ❁❁ *One mile north of Cahuita on Black Beach; tel. and fax (506) 755-0035. Mail: Apdo. 1132, Puerto Limón.* Casually elegant bed and breakfast. Comfortable rooms have ceiling fans (no air conditioning) and large tiled patios, also with ceiling fans. The pool, set among coral and flowering gardens, is a delightful oasis. 6 rooms. Major credit cards.

Best Western Punta Cocles ✿✿✿ *South of Puerto Viejo; tel. (506) 234-8055, fax (506) 234-8033. Mail: Apdo. 11020-1000, San José.* Large, clean rooms, all with air-conditioning, some with kitchenettes. The open-air restaurant has an extensive local menu. Private rain forest and lots of wildlife on the property. The beach is within walking distance; there's also an outdoor pool and children's playground. 60 rooms. Major credit cards.

Maribu Caribe Hotel ✿✿✿ *Puerto Limón; tel. (506) 758-4543, fax (506) 758-3541. Mail: Apdo. 623-7300, Puerto Limón.* Set atop a seaside bluff with great views of the Caribbean. No direct access to the beach, but the water is only a 10-minute walk away. Facilities include a top-notch outdoor restaurant and swimming pool. Large rooms have queen-sized beds and air-conditioning. 52 rooms. Major credit cards.

Villas de Caribe ✿✿✿ *Puerto Viejo; tel. (506) 233-2200, fax (506) 221-2801. Mail: Apdo. 8080-1000, San José.* Just a stone's throw away from the beach, this small hotel is one of the nicest in the Puerto Viejo area. Large, comfortable two-story villas with kitchenettes. Set in a small nature preserve with lots of rain-forest birds. 12 rooms. Major credit cards.

Caribbean Coast North (Tortuguero, Barra del Colorado)

Tortuga Lodge ✿✿✿✿ *Tortuguero; tel. (506) 257-0766, fax (506) 257-1665. Mail: Apdo. 6941-1000, San José.* Probably the most luxurious accommodation and best food in Tortuguero. Run by Costa Rica Expeditions, who bring a lot of experience and professionalism to the operation. Canal tour boats use environment- and manatee-friendly electric motors. 25 rooms. Major credit cards.

Mawamba Lodge ✿✿✿ *Tortuguero; tel. (506) 223-7490, fax (506) 255-4039. Mail: Apdo. 10050-1000, San José.* Very near Tortuguero village, but far enough away so there's no noise. Beautiful gardens surround the rooms, with wildlife coming and going throughout the day. No air-conditioning, but all rooms have fans. Swimming pool and Jacuzzi. Patio dining offering excellent local and Continental cuisine. Rates include transportation to and from the lodge, tours, and three meals a day. 40 rooms. Major credit cards.

Pacific Coast (Puntarenas Vicinity)

Caribbean Village Fiesta Hotel ✿✿✿✿ *Just south of Puntarenas; tel. (506) 663-0808, fax (506) 663-1516. Mail: Apdo. 171-5400, Puntarenas.* Recently rechristened and gone the "all-inclusive" route, the Fiesta features large rooms and suites, satellite TV, and all the other amenities of a modern beach resort. There are several restaurants and bars, and a casino for those who like gaming. Close to San José and cruise-ship ports. Wheelchair access. 220 rooms. Major credit cards.

Villa Caletas ✿✿✿✿ *Off the main road, 21 miles south of Puntarenas, 5 miles north of Playa Jacó; tel. (506) 257-3653, fax (506) 222-2059. Mail: Apdo. 12358-1000, San José.* Luxurious large rooms and private villas, and perhaps the best Pacific Ocean views are to be found from this hillside perch. Legendary sunsets. Gorgeous free-form pool appears to blend in with the ocean below. 28 rooms. Major credit cards.

Pacific Coast (Guanacaste, Santa Rosa National Park)

Costa Smeralda ✿✿✿✿ *Playa Panamá, Guanacaste Province; tel. (506) 670-0044, fax (506) 670-0379. Mail: Apdo. 12177-1000, San José.* Luxurious all-inclusive resort, with all the amenities. Rooms have great views from spacious patios. The open-air restaurant features French and Italian cuisine. Swimming, tennis, and snorkeling are just a few of the activities. 88 rooms. Major credit cards.

Hotel Las Espuelas ✿✿ *On the Inter-American Highway, just south of Liberia; tel. (506) 239-2000, fax (506) 239-2405. Mail: Apdo. 88-5000, Liberia.* With its hacienda styling, beautiful gardens, giant old shade trees, and clean, cosy rooms, this is probably the nicest hotel in the Liberia area. A swimming pool and casino are included in the facilities. Guanacaste beaches and Rincón de la Vieja National Park are about 40 minutes away. 44 rooms. Major credit cards.

Hotel Hacienda La Pacífica ✿✿✿ *On the Inter-American Highway, in Cañas, Guanacaste; tel. (506) 669-0266, fax (506) 669-0555. Mail: Apdo. 8-5700, Cañas, Guanacaste.* Located on the banks of the Corobicí river, 25 miles south of Liberia, this comfortable spread is a good base for tours and adventures, and breaks up the long drive to or from the Guanacaste beaches. 33 rooms. Major credit cards.

Aurola Playa Flamingo Holiday Inn ✿✿✿✿ *Playa Flamingo, Guanacaste; tel. (506) 233-7233, fax (506) 255-1171. Mail: Apdo. 7802-1000, San José.* Modern high-rise luxury hotel on a beautiful white-sand beach. Large pool and poolside restaurant. Small gym, game room. Easy access to good sport fishing and scuba diving. Wheelchair access. 88 rooms. Major credit cards.

Meliá Playa Conchal ✿✿✿✿ *On Playa Conchal Beach in Guanacaste Province; tel. (506) 654-4123, fax (506) 654-4181. Mail: Apdo. 232-5150, Santa Cruz, Guanacaste.* Large-scale luxury resort on a beautiful crushed-shell beach. All rooms are suites with all the modern amenities. Tennis courts, golf course, health club, water sports, activities, and a gigantic pool. Several restaurants and bars. 310 suites. Major credit cards.

Pacific Coast (Nicoya Peninsula)

Barceló Playa Tambor ✿✿✿✿ *On Playa Tambor, Nicoya Peninsula; tel. (506) 683-0303, fax (506) 683-0304. Mail: Apdo. 771-1150, La Uruca San José.* All-inclusive resort, with plenty of activities and amenities. All rooms have terraces or balconies, and some offer ocean views. Facilities include a swimming pool, Jacuzzi, tennis courts, and golf course (opening in 1999). 402 rooms. Major credit cards.

Hotel Punta Islita ❁❁❁❁ *Northwest coast of Nicoya Peninsula; tel. (506) 231-6122, fax (506) 231-0715. Mail: Apdo. 6054-1000 San José.* Hillside setting provides great views of the Pacific. Large, comfortable rooms all have private patios that take in the view. Some even come with a Jacuzzi. Facilities include a swimming pool, fitness center, and tennis courts, plus a gourmet open-air restaurant with giant thatched roof. 25 rooms. Major credit cards.

Pacific Coast (Near Manuel Antonio National Park)

Makanda-By-The-Sea ❁❁❁❁ *Off the road to Manuel Antonio Beach; tel. (506) 777-0442, fax (506) 777-1032. Mail: Apdo. 29, Quepos.* Elegant private villas come in a variety of size and shapes. Inviting pool and Jacuzzi. Excellent nouvelle-cuisine dinners served under cloth tents pool-side. Continental breakfast delivered to your room. 7 rooms. Major credit cards.

Hotel & Villas Si Como No ❁❁❁❁ *On the road to Manuel Antonio Beach; tel. (506) 777-0777, fax (506) 777-1093. Mail: Apdo. 5-6350, Quepos.* Mostly suites with king- or queen-sized beds; all with private balcony and coastline view. Everything here is ecologically conscious, right down to the farm-grown wood used in construction. Inviting pool, with swim-up bar, slide, waterfall, and Jacuzzi. There's also a small private theatre for nightly movies. 39 rooms. Major credit cards.

Verde Del Mar ❁❁ *Manuel Antonio; tel. (506) 777-1805, fax (506) 777-1311. Mail: Apdo. 348-6350, Quepos.* One of the only true beach hotels in Manuel Antonio. Comfortable rooms in various categories; some with air conditioning, some with kitchenettes. 20 rooms. Major credit cards.

Pacific Coast (Near Carara Biological Reserve)

Villas Lapas ❁❁❁❁ *Tarcoles, Puntarenas; tel. (506) 663-0811, fax (506) 663-1516. Mail: Apdo. 419-4005, Puntarenas.* Situated on the banks of the Río Tarcoles on the edge of Carara Biological Reserve. Rooms are large, private, and all open onto a shady verandah. Some have air-conditioning, others only fans. An all-inclusive resort for eco-travelers; you can watch the scarlet macaws from the large open-air restaurant and decks. Pool, butterfly garden, and miniature golf round out the amenities. 47 rooms. Major credit cards.

Pacific Coast (Near Corcovado National Park)

Bosque del Cabo Wilderness Lodge ❁❁❁❁ *Osa Peninsula; tel. (506) 735-5062, fax (506) 735-5043. Mail: Puerto Jiménez, Osa Peninsula (in Costa Rica); in U.S., Interlink 528, P.O. Box 025635, Miami, FL 33152.* Rustic luxury in thatched or tile-roofed cabins with private ocean-view porches. Beach is within walking distance and dense rain forest is all around. All meals included in rates. 7 rooms. Visa or cash only.

Lapa Rios ❁❁❁❁ *Osa Peninsula; tel. (506) 735-5130, fax (506) 735-5179. Mail: Apdo. 100, Puerto Jiménez, Osa Peninsula; in U.S., P.O. Box 025216, Miami, FL 33102.* Surrounded by its own huge rain forest preserve, this luxury resort is one of the nicest in Costa Rica. Totally private. Huge rooms with private deck (expansive ocean and rain forest views) and outdoor shower. No TV, telephone, or air-conditioning, but lots of wildlife, tours, and activities. Rates include meals. 14 rooms. Major credit cards.

Pacific Coast (Monteverde Region)

Arco Iris Lodge ❁ *Monteverde; tel. (506) 645-5067, fax (506) 645-5022. Mail: Apdo. 003-5655, Monteverde, Puntarenas.* Rare budget gem on the edge of Santa Elena village. Clean, comfortable rooms, attentive service, and well-tended grounds. 9 rooms. Visa only.

Monteverde Lodge ❁❁ *Monteverede; tel. (506) 257-0766, fax (506) 257-1665. Mail: Apdo. 6941-1000, San José.* An upscale hotel surrounded by groomed gardens and cloud forest, with overview of the valley below. Close to both Santa Elena and the Monteverde Cloud Forest Reserve. Rooms are comfortable, with large windows that let nature in. A large Jacuzzi near the lobby lets hikers soak out their aches and pains. Wheelchair access. 27 rooms. Major credit cards.

Arenal Region

Arenal Observatory Lodge ❁❁ *On the flanks of Arenal Volcano; tel. (506) 257-9489, fax (506) 257-4220. Mail: Apdo. 321-1007, Centro Colón, San José.* Originally a research center for the study of Arenal Volcano, this hotel has beautiful views of the cone and Arenal Lake. The nicest rooms have walls of glass for viewing the nighttime eruptions. Rain-forest trails and guided tours. 28 rooms. Major credit cards.

Tabacón Lodge ❁❁❁❁ *On the road between La Fortuna and Arenal Volcano; tel. (506) 256-1500, fax (506) 221-3076. Mail: Apdo. 181-1007, Centro Colón, San José.* New luxury hotel faces the volcano and is just across the street from the steaming mineral pools and gardens of the Tabacón Hot Springs. Rooms are large and most have direct views of the volcanic cone. Wheelchair access. 42 rooms. Major credit cards.

Tilajari Hotel & Resort ❁❁❁ *Muelle, San Carlos; tel. (506) 469-9091, fax (506) 469-9095. Mail: Apdo. 81-4100, San Carlos.* Set in a small nature preserve on the banks of the San Carlos river, with tennis courts, two pools, a butterfly garden, and other adventures and tours. Rooms are spacious; the best ones have river views. Wheelchair access. 64 rooms. Major credit cards.

Recommended Restaurants

When choosing a restaurant, a standard rule of thumb is simply to go where the locals go, then eat what the locals eat. If you don't know, ask. Anyone can tell you, from a hotel desk clerk to the man or woman on the street. Reservations are generally required only at the higher-end restaurants, and even then only during the high season and on weekends.

Breakfast is usually served from 6 or 6:30 A.M. until 8 or 10 A.M.; lunch is usually served between 11 A.M. or noon and 2 or 3 P.M.; dinner is usually served from 6 P.M. until 9 or 10 P.M. Even if a restaurant serves all meals, it often closes in the late morning before the lunch service and in the late afternoon before the dinner service; occasionally, you will find establishments with continual service and those that are open quite late. We give specific hours for restaurants only when they do not fit within these parameters.

Prices below are per person, for a full meal with beverage.

✿✿✿	U.S.$25 and up
✿✿	U.S.$10–$25
✿	Less than U.S.$10

San José

La Piazzetta ✿✿ *Paseo Colón near Calle 40; tel. (506) 222-7896.* Lunch and dinner. Closed Sunday. A fairly formal Italian restaurant (by Costa Rican standards), with a number of exotic Italian dishes you don't often find elsewhere. Risotto, fresh seafood. Major credit cards.

Café Parisien ✿✿ *Gran Hotel Costa Rica, Avenida 2 between Calles 1 and 3; tel. (506) 221-4011.* Open 24 hours daily. Situated under a covered verandah in front of the Gran Hotel adjacent to the Plaza Cultura, the Café Parisien serves excellent Costa Rican and American food and is a great place to watch the world go by, day or night. Major credit cards.

La Cocina De Leña ✿✿ *Centro Comercial El Pueblo; tel. (506) 255-1360.* Open daily 11 A.M.–11 P.M. A family-owned business, La Cocina De Leña is decorated like a colonial farmhouse, with wall candles, tile floors, red tablecloths, an open kitchen, fresh stalks of plantains, and bundles of firewood to feed the restaurant's namesake wood stove. The *gallo pinto* with fried plantains and hot salsa is great, as is the *olla de carne,* an oversized bowl of beef, steamed corn, and potatoes. Major credit cards.

La Esmeralda ✿ *Avenida 2 between Calles 5 and 7; tel. (506) 221-0530.* Open for lunch and dinner, sometimes until 5 A.M. Closed Sunday. Numerous full-scale Mariachi ensembles roam around and play for pay. The cavernous room has worn, red tables, wooden chairs, and large oil paintings, and as a people-watching spot this ranks right alongside the Café Parisien. Free plates of *bocas* (beans, chips, and sausage hunks in a spicy sauce) accompanying the drinks are part of the appeal, and the Costa Rican food is excellent. Major credit cards.

Machu Pichu Bar and Restaurant ✿✿ *Calle 32, between Avenida 1 and Avenida 3; tel. (506) 222-7384.* Open for lunch and dinner to 10 P.M. Closed Sunday. A 17-table, hole-in-the-wall that serves some of the best Peruvian food in Central America. The seafood platter is a house speciality prepared for two. Major credit cards.

Manolo's Restaurante ✿ *Avenida Central between Calles Central and 2; tel. (506) 221-2041.* Open 24 hours daily. This is sort of a combination Costa Rican coffee shop and diner. Still, the pastries, soups, sandwiches, and everyday Tico food is top-notch. Located in the heart of downtown. Major credit cards.

Café Mundo ✿✿ *Calle 15 and Avenida 9; tel. (506) 222-6190.* Open for lunch and dinner to 11 P.M. or midnight on weekends. Closed lunch Saturday, all day Sunday. You'll find seating in every nook and cranny of this restored colonial mansion, including the garden patios and covered verandahs. Creative

Continental cuisine, with daily specials and incredible desserts. Major credit cards.

La Isabela ✿✿✿ *At the Marriott Hotel and Resort, San Antonio de Belén; tel. (506) 298-0000.* Dinner only. One of the most elegant restaurants in the country, serving fine Continental and nouvelle Costa Rican cuisine, in a wine-cellar environment, with arched ceilings and low lighting. Only 15 tables here, so reservations are recommended. Major credit cards.

La Luz ✿✿✿ *Calle Vieja to Santa Ana; tel. (506) 282-4160.* Open daily from 7 A.M. Located inside the boutique Hotel Alta, this restaurant serves some of the most creative food in Costa Rica, mixing local ingredients with Pacific-Rim and Southwestern-American fusion cuisines. Elegant setting and formal service in a spacious room with walls of glass overlooking the Central Valley. Major credit cards.

La Masía de Triquel ✿✿✿ *175 metres west and 175 metres north of the Datsun Agency, Sabana Norte; tel. (506) 296-3528.* Closed Sunday. Specialities include lamb and rabbit dishes, as well as traditional Spanish seafood favourites, and of course paella. Elegant service and ambiance. Major credit cards.

Ruiseñor Café ✿✿ *Avenida 2 between Calles 3 and 5; tel. 506/256-6094.* Open 10:30 A.M.–6 P.M.; closed Sunday. Located in the lobby of the beautiful National Theatre, this is a great place for lunch, early dinner, or a coffee and dessert. High ceilings sport Neo-Classical fresco paintings. Continental cuisine, hearty sandwiches, fresh quîche and plenty of home-baked goodies. Major credit cards.

Escazú

Atlanta Dining Gallery ✿✿ *Hotel Tara, Escazú; tel. (506) 228-6992.* Open daily from 7 A.M. Located in a colonial mansion in the hills above San José, Hotel Tara is an homage to "Gone With The Wind." The formal dining room has a wood-burning fireplace,

Costa Rican art, and tables set with sparkling crystal and fresh-cut flowers. French and Costa Rican chefs prepare a chicken dish in a curry sauce with raisins and coconuts that will make your palate gloat. The views are spectacular. Major credit cards.

San Pedro

Ambrosia ❁❁ *Centro Comercial Calle Real; tel. (506) 253-8012.* Open for lunch and dinner; Sunday for lunch only. You'll find no better steaks or seafood, all prepared with a Continental flair, in the Central Valley. Major credit cards.

Puerto Limón

Restaurant Hotel Maribu Caribe ❁❁ *Calle Portete 3 km (2 miles) northwest of Puerto Limón; tel. (506) 758-4543.* Open daily from 7 A.M. The open-air restaurant in this pleasant hotel overlooking the sea serves tasty Costa Rican dishes with a Caribbean flair. Major credit cards.

Restaurant Hotel Matama ❁❁ *Calle Portete 3½ km (2¼ miles) northwest of Puerto Limón; tel. (506) 758-1123.* Open daily from 7 A.M. Like most good eateries on the Caribbean coast, this one has a large, open-air dining room. You'll be surrounded by lush gardens and the sounds of frolicking birds. The speciality here is seafood, fresh from the boats in Puerto Limón. Major credit cards.

Cahuita

Miss Edith's Restaurant ❁ *Downtown Cahuita; tel. (506) 755-0248.* Usually open daily from 7 A.M., for dinner only Sunday (usually shorter hours during the low season). A family operation (right down to the long, multi-person tables) where mom cooks while the kids wait tables. The specialities here are all Creole seafood, most of them spicy. Cash only.

Casa Creole ❁❁ *Playa Negra road, at Magellan Inn; tel. (506) 755-0104.* Dinner only; closed Sunday. Elegant open-air dining on linen tablecloths in a typical pastel pink and gingerbread-trimmed Caribbean house. The cuisine blends French and Caribbean influences with plenty of fresh fish and homemade desserts. Major credit cards.

Puerto Viejo

The Garden Restaurant ❁❁ *At Cabinas Jacaranda; tel. (506) 750-0069.* Open from 6 A.M.; closed Tuesday and often for long stretches in spring and fall. Located two blocks from the center of Puerto Viejo, this is one of the most eclectic and satisfying restaurants in all of Costa Rica. With a mix of Caribbean, Asian, and local cuisines. Visa only.

Puntarenas

Bierstube ❁❁ *Paseo de los Turistas between Calles 21 and 23; tel. (506) 661-0330.* Open for lunch and dinner to midnight; closed Monday. This loud, lively, and spacious "beer garden" serves copious amounts of local brew, alongside good steak and seafood dishes. Window seats get you a fresh breeze and view of the Golfo de Nicoya. Major credit cards.

La Caravelle ❁❁ *Paseo de los Turistas between Calles 21 and 23; tel. (506) 661-2262.* Open for lunch and dinner; closed Monday and Tuesday. A traditional French restaurant offering some truly fine beef and seafood dishes. The fish will always be fresh. A good choice is the *camarónes a la mantequilla y limón* (shrimp with butter and lemon). Major credit cards.

El Mirador/El Anfiteatro ❁❁❁ *At Villa Caletas, off the main road 35 km (21 miles) south of Puntarenas, 8 km (5 miles) north of Playa Jacó; tel. (506) 257-3653.* Open daily. A mix of fine French, Continental and nouvelle Costa Rican cuisine served alongside arguably the most stunning view in the whole country. Open air, yet extremely elegant dining. Major credit cards.

Liberia (Santa Rosa National Park) and Vicinity

Pókopí Restaurant ❁❁ *On the road west to Santa Cruz near the El Sitio Hotel; tel. (506) 666-1036.* Open for lunch and dinner daily. Small, but a real treat where fresh fish, steaks, and chicken are concerned. A disco gets cranking most nights after 10 P.M. Major credit cards.

Restaurant Hotel Las Espuelas ✪✪ *At the Hotel Las Espuelas, Inter-American Highway; tel. (506) 239-2000.* Open daily from 7 A.M. Typical Costa Rican food is the specialty here, with a mix of Continental thrown in for good measure. The seafood is all fresh. Major credit cards.

Guanacaste (Northern Beaches)

Marie's ✪✪ *Near the Flamingo Marina Hotel, Playa Flamingo; tel. (506) 654-4136.* Open daily from 6:30 A.M. Fresh seafood perfectly prepared is the speciality here. Open-air, casual atmosphere. Visa or cash only.

Playa de Los Artistas ✪✪ *Across from Hotel Los Mangos, Montezuma; tel. (506) 661-2550.* Open for dinner only; closed Sunday. A few large cross-sectional timber tables sit on sand under a low tin roof. Every thing is lit by candlelight. Excellent Mediterranean-style fare. Worth the drive if you're staying at Playa Tambor. Cash only.

Quepos (Manuel Antonio National Park)

Barba Roja ✪✪ *Road to Manuel Antonio 2 km (1 mile) from Quepos; tel. (506) 777-0331.* Open from 7 A.M.; Monday for dinner only. A favourite among knowledgeable locals. Their portions are gigantic and the homemade nachos are out of this world. Dining is casual in a large open-air room, with high ceilings and a bit of an ocean view. Visa or cash only.

El Gran Escape ✪✪ *Downtown Quepos; tel. (506) 777-0395.* Open from 6 A.M.; closed Tuesday. Popular local restaurant and bar serves the freshest fish along this stretch of coast. Major credit cards.

Plinio ❁❁ *About 1 km (½ mile) from Quepos on the road to Manuel Antonio National Park; tel. (506) 777-0055.* Open for breakfast and dinner daily. Italian food is the speciality of the house. Although you have to climb some steps to get here, you'll enjoy the open-air balcony dining. Major credit cards.

Monteverde Region

Restaurante De Lucía ❁❁ *On the road to the Butterfly Farm, Monteverde; tel. (506) 645-5337.* Open daily for lunch and dinner. You choose your cut of chicken or meat or your fish from a platter and they cook it to order. The atmosphere is casual and friendly. Major credit cards.

Monteverde Lodge Restaurant ❁❁ *In the Monteverde Lodge, on a side road just outside of Santa Elena; tel. (506) 257-0766.* Open daily from 6 A.M. Sunsets and views of the surrounding forest are excellent from the dining room here. There's a small nightly selection of Costa Rican and Continental dishes on the menu, all of them tasty. Whether or not you are staying here, reservations are recommended. Major credit cards.

El Sapo Dorado Restaurant ❁❁ *On the road between Santa Elena Village and Monteverde; tel. (506) 645-5010.* Open daily from 6:30 A.M. The chef here has imagination, so the seafood and Continental and Costa Rican cuisine is served with a little something special in the way of sauces and spices. On a clear day the views to the west are exceptional, especially around sunset. Major credit cards.

Arenal Region

Ave del Paraiso ❁❁ *On the road from La Fortuna to Arenal Volcano, at Tabacón Spa; tel. (506) 256-1500.* Open daily from 7 A.M. This beautiful open-air restaurant overlooks the steaming mineral pools and rain-forest gardens of the Tabacón Hot Springs, with views of Arenal Volcano. Well-prepared Costa Rican and Italian cuisine is served. Major credit cards.

ABOUT BERLITZ

In 1878 Professor Maximilian Berlitz had a revolutionary idea about making language learning accessible and enjoyable. One hundred and twenty years later these same principles are still successfully at work.

For language instruction, translation and interpretation services, cross-cultural training, study abroad programs, and an array of publishing products and additional services, visit any one of our more than 350 Berlitz Centers in over 40 countries.

Please consult your local telephone directory for the Berlitz Center nearest you or visit our web site at http://www.berlitz.com.

Helping the World Communicate